Only Connect

The Difficult Second Quiz Book

Only Connect

The Difficult Second Quiz Book

JACK WALEY-COHEN
AND DAVID McGAUGHEY

INTRODUCTION BY
VICTORIA COREN MITCHELL

BOOKS

BBC Books, an imprint of Ebury Publishing
20 Vauxhall Bridge Road,
London SW1V 2SA

BBC Books is part of the Penguin Random House group of companies
whose addresses can be found at global.penguinrandomhouse.com

Penguin
Random House
UK

First published by BBC Books in 2019
Paperback edition published by BBC Books in 2020

www.penguin.co.uk

A CIP catalogue record for this book is available from the British Library

ISBN 9781785944598

Printed and bound in Great Britain by Clays Ltd, Elcograf S.p.A.

Penguin Random House is committed to a sustainable future for
our business, our readers and our planet. This book is made
from Forest Stewardship Council® certified paper.

MIX
Paper from
responsible sources
FSC® C018179

CONTENTS

INTRODUCTION

by Victoria Coren Mitchell

Hello again. My, aren't you a glutton for punishment?

I assume you've watched *Only Connect* on television and feel ready to address its complexities in a different medium. Perhaps you have read our first quiz book and are relishing the idea of a second. Either way, you've kidded yourself that you enjoyed a previous gruelling exercise in masochism so you're reaching for another. I understand completely. I used to smoke.

I wonder who you are? I've met a fair few quizzers in my time. Do you have a healthy appetite for acquiring new facts and a good memory for retaining them? Do you have no general knowledge

INTRODUCTION

but a strong capacity for lateral thinking? Are you simply ready to gamble? Maybe it's none of the above but you enjoy failure, just as Dostoevsky got a thrill from losing at roulette.

Can you do all four rounds of Only Connect? Do you come alive for the music question, or block your ears and wait for the next one? Do you love the sequences? Or perhaps you can only do the missing vowels.

Are you dark or fair? Deep-voiced or squeaky? Ticklish? Long-sighted? Bald? If you appeared on the actual programme, would you wear a plain pastel shirt, a funny T-shirt or a ballgown? Odd socks, spangly shoes, lucky pants?

I wonder whether you're a light-hearted quizzer or a stern and sombre one. As part of a team, are you the type to insist you know the answer when you're only 60% sure – or, when quite certain, do you silently cuddle the truth to yourself because you hate overruling a colleague? Are you frightened of spiders? Buttons? Elbows? Quizzes? Cheese?

Most importantly, what are your best key facts?

When I introduce our teams at the start of each episode, I always give a fact or two about each player. Sometimes they're a bit unusual or surprising, even funny; sometimes perfectly ordinary. What amazes me is how often I am asked by viewers: "Are the 'team facts' true, or do you invent them?"

Of course they're true! Why would we need to invent things about people when we can simply ask them about themselves? Truth is stranger than fiction, after all. The premise of any quiz is that we live in an intriguing world and our environment bears close examination. Every person on God's good earth is interesting. If you don't agree, you are not a true quizzer. (Either that or you've sat next to me at dinner after one gin too many.)

Everything I say on screen about our contestants has come out in conversation between them and our assistant producer, Hannah-Jane Davies. They have a wide-ranging, soul-searching chat. Hannah takes the resulting list of facts to our producer, Jenny Heap, for another chat.

(Yes, two women in those senior roles. Also, the director of *Only Connect*, the production manager and the owners of Parasol Media, the company that makes the show, are female. All female and all Welsh; trust me, it's a chatty production.)

So they chat, Jenny selects and writes up the final facts, Hannah brings them to me in the makeup chair, I say, "I can't possibly read that aloud with a straight face" and on we go.

Sometimes, the teams are grilled for extra facts. Sometimes, I re-word them. Jenny is a good sounding board because her brain works differently from mine. She's very clever, but 0% of her brain is scanning for accidental filth. It just doesn't occur to her.

INTRODUCTION

One time, reading through the proposed descriptions of upcoming teams, I shrieked: "I can't say 'He enjoys tinkering with his collection'! Where do you think the viewers will look when he stands up for the wall round?"

Another time, when I baulked at the line 'He spends most of his time tending his mother's smallholding', Jenny literally couldn't see what the problem was. And I certainly wasn't going to spell it out, so we left it as was. (If you're the quizzer I so described on BBC Two at 8.30pm, no disrespect intended by this story. It's a lovely way to spend your time.)

The team facts can provide a fun, efficient shortcut into a newcomer's personality. Collectively, they reflect our *Only Connect* world of eclectic interests and idiosyncratic lives. But many of our contestants, although appearing on TV for the show, are shy, private people; cleverly chosen, the facts can do just as good a job of *obscuring* them. It just depends what they elect to tell Hannah.

For example, if I were going on *Only Connect* as a contestant and I was happy for viewers to get to know me, I might allow a description such as:

"Victoria, an English graduate who's unafraid of gambling or public speaking, but terrified of almost everything else."

or

> "Victoria, a geriatric mother who sneezes for the first four hours of every day and speaks excellent French."

or

> "Victoria, a fussy eater and comedy fan who failed her first driving test because she crashed the car into some roadworks."

or

> "Victoria, a short-tempered ex-smoker who once spent twenty minutes trimming matted fur off the backside of someone else's cat."

Any of those options would lay my soul bare pretty quickly. However, it would be equally true but far less revealing to describe me as:

> "Victoria, a Londoner who's been to Timbuktu."

or

> "Victoria, who won the prize for Best Sponge Cake at the 2006 Clacton Arts Festival."

or

> *"Victoria, who once sat behind Peter Bowles on a*
> *flight to Edinburgh."*

Those latter facts obscure more than they reveal. I don't know why. The last three Victorias could be spies. The first four couldn't. But they're all me.

In this book, straight after this introductory essay, you will find a selection of some of the facts we have used to describe contestants over the years. The listed names weren't chosen because they're particularly more interesting than the others. *Everyone is interesting*. (And *Only Connect* contestants are more interesting than most.) But, to give a flavour of the wonderful people who have passed through our hallowed Welsh doors, I thought it would be nice to include a random selection of their introductory facts. I suggest you read it all in one go like a poem.

• • •

After "Let's meet the teams", you will find a series of complete *Only Connect* games to play. There are nine in total: the first three games are, roughly, "opening heat" level, the next three are "quarter and semi final" level and the last three are demoralizingly difficult. If you score well on those, come on the show! I'm serious.

All the questions in these games have been broadcast at some point in our 11-year life, but they have never been grouped in this way. Near the end of the book, you will also find a chunky batch of connecting walls and missing vowel clues that have never been broadcast so will be entirely unfamiliar to you. (As will the questions in the first nine games, if your brain is anything like mine).

* * *

In between each game, like a delicious sorbet to cleanse the palate, you will find a memory from one of the special guest quizzers who have at some point come along to Cardiff to take part in one-off charity episodes for Children In Need, Comic Relief or Sport Relief.

Those episodes grew out of an earlier suggestion from somebody at the BBC to make "celebrity specials", a phrase which caused me to shiver with trepidation. No disrespect to any of the excellent TV quizzes which offer very entertaining celebrity versions, but the concept seemed at odds with our *Only Connect* world. It smacked of a different cultural register, even a different value system.

We were, after all, on BBC Four, a channel which didn't go in much for quizzes (or light entertainment at all.) We were meant to *be* the light entertainment, and we owe a large vote of thanks to some early visionaries at BBC Four for opening the door to that.

Many of our viewers had fled to the channel as a refuge from the makeover programmes, talent contests and "reality shows" of terrestrial television. These viewers rolled up at the BBC's shy, cultish fourth channel in hope of finding a gripping documentary about bi-planes, an imported Danish drama or an experimental six-hour music recital.

When *Only Connect* began, they were patient and welcoming – perhaps recognising that we deferred to their frame of reference and intellectual curiosity. Or perhaps they just mistook our low-budget set and my cheap clothes for scholarliness.

I thought it might be testing their patience a little much to wheel out a load of *Heat* magazine regulars to play the connecting wall and call it a treat. I worried about the implication that it was more "special" to have WAGs or pop singers than science teachers, librarians or hospital registrars. *Only Connect* wasn't a razzle-dazzle show; if we suddenly appeared to be shouting, "Never mind all those second-hand book dealers, finally someone off *Hollyoaks* is here!", our viewers might feel betrayed.

Besides, I reasoned, those people just *wouldn't be able to do it*. It would take more drinks than you can afford for me to tell you the list of names that were originally put forward as prospective "celebrity quizzers", but let's just say they did not strike me as people who'd be quick to put the noble gases in alphabetical order. (I did think it might make a hilarious *Comic Relief* episode to invite them all on and watch them score 0, but it would be a joke of

which our guests would not have been in control.
It wouldn't have been fair.)

I mean, almost nobody can do this quiz! If I watch
it on television, I barely score a point and I was there
when we recorded it!

So we agreed instead to make a few charity
specials, rejecting the proposed list of contestants
(who'd been mooted purely on grounds of fame) and
head-hunting instead for those in the public eye that
we thought were *likely to be good quizzers*. Or, perhaps
more importantly, that our *loyal viewers* would think
were likely to be good quizzers.

We weren't always right. Professor Steve Jones,
for example, is one of the most brilliant men of his
generation, an eminent and celebrated geneticist; a
proper genius and, better still, Welsh. However, he
was something of a novice quizzer.

BUZZ! "Are they all hats?"

"Well ... no, but also we need to know *what comes
next in the sequence*.."

"Oh right! My mistake! Let's start again!"

"We can't start again, Professor, it's a competitive
quiz..."

Nevertheless, it was an honour to meet him
(though I deeply regret learning that snails feel
pain, which he told me gloomily over lunch); he
was lovely to spend time with and his presence,
along with that of Professor Susan Greenfield, Sir
Andrew Motion, Julian Lloyd-Webber, Rosie Boycott,

INTRODUCTION

Michael Bywater, Simon Singh, Patrick Marber, Samira Ahmed, Clemency Burton-Hill, Matthew Parris, Ian Hislop and many other sparkling guest quizzers, managed to meet the brief of introducing a few recognised names without making our regular viewers feel we'd lost all sense of reason and priority.

A randomly-invited nine of those special guest players will crop up between the games here, sharing questions they remember from their charity episodes and revealing whether they got the answers right or wrong. I won't tell you who they are, but I will tell you (1) they include none of the above and (2) they do include

A writer and cartoonist who got married in Las Vegas and once had to actively stop himself from talking too much about pine cones

A horseracing expert who's directly descended from Henry VII and was suspended from school for shoplifting

And

A fossil collector and skilled portrait painter, who built a fully-equipped Victorian laboratory in his house.

So those are the kind of people we like to have around. If you do too, then you're going to enjoy this book immensely!

Good luck.

Victoria Coren Mitchell

Let's Meet the Teams

- Joanna Murray, a Durham maths graduate who plays the ukulele, and has won a competition to design a pavement sweeper;
- Amy Godel, an expert macaroon baker who, despite many challenges and against all odds, successfully delivered a mobile dentist to the Channel Islands;
- Mark Oxley, a physiotherapist who works for the Toulouse rugby league team, though he has never visited Toulouse;
- Min Lacey, a civil servant who loves amateur dramatics, Snoopy and Dick Francis;
- Chris Pendleton, an artist and picture framer who is commissioned annually to paint a picture of a pig for Britain's leading sausage manufacturer;
- Andrew Burford, a Black Country ombudsman who once ate his own height in sandwiches;
- Sam Goodyear, a history graduate who now works as a futures trader and played trumpet at Pete Postlethwaite's stag night;
- Taissa Csáky, a classics graduate whose dog, Zephyr, bears a striking resemblance to Anubis, the Egyptian god of the afterlife;
- Tom Chisholm, a history graduate who was given a box of satsumas by Tom Stoppard;
- Paul Richardson, a retired fire officer who had

a lengthy conversation with Princess Anne about the problems with the M6 motorway around Preston;

- George Corfield, a cryptic crossworder who has dated two women suffering from typhoid;
- Hannah Hogben, a chemistry graduate who's written an award-winning song about a squid;
- Chris White, a politics and economics student whose dream job would be driving steam trains;
- Kirsty Johnston, a deputy partnership accountant who loves Enid Blyton novels and knits jumpers for battery chickens;
- Paddy Duffy, an author and former youth worker who once invited an Irish cabinet minister to the cinema by accident;
- David Brewis, a schoolmaster who enjoys knitting and is studying to be a London cab driver;
- Andy Ross, a music guru, writer and band manager, and the man who discovered Blur;
- Richard Heald, a native Yorkshireman who has bottle fed a sheep in Britain's highest pub;
- Andrew Frazer, a Company Director and former civil servant who shook Margaret Thatcher's hand while dressed as a fifty pence piece;
- Tom Scott, a linguistics graduate who also runs the British 'Talk Like a Pirate' day;
- Liz Scott-Wilson, an information architect for a leading London law firm who won New Zealand's *University Challenge* in 1981;

- Frank Paul, an artist and pub quiz host who was surprised by an intimate prophecy while sketching a camel;
- Nick Atty, a civil servant with PhD in Genetics, who has written a software program for British canal routes;
- Jean Upton, a photographer and former yoga instructor who once shared a bottle of Southern Comfort with Janis Joplin;
- Shreeya Nanda, a bio-medical editor with a specialist knowledge of the testes of the fruit fly;
- Justin Floyd, a history graduate who hails from Georgia and boasts a significant collection of ceramic dog figurines;
- Fergus Butler-Gallie, an Oxford University student and former bishop's assistant who enjoys rugby, beer, gin and church;
- Owen Rees, a music teacher who can juggle and play the trombone at the same time and has carved a ham for Sir Antony Hopkins;
- Chris Grandison, a hospital administrator whose happiest memory is a 15-second glimpse of a kingfisher;
- Annette Fenner, a travel enthusiast who honeymooned in Syria and can only write upside down;
- Jamie Turner, a highway engineer who once sold a pair of trainers to the poet Simon Armitage;

- Michael Jelley, a wine merchant who received the only yellow card in the history of Leicestershire's under-nine's football;
- Tony Moore, a foster carer who inadvertently became part of the entourage of King Albert II while holidaying in Belgium;
- Emily Watnick, a retired finance manager and history enthusiast who discovered a medieval anthrax pit during a routine archaeological dig;
- Mark Wallace, a political journalist who got into an altercation with global megastar Seal over an egg and cress sandwich;
- Mike Arrowsmith, a university computer officer who has been chased up the longest escalator in Europe by Czech riot police;
- Nick Lister, a fraud prevention specialist who knows the words to 'Around the World with Willy Fog' in five different languages;
- Charlotte Jackson, an epidemiologist who has appeared on Kuwaiti telvision;
- Vikki Nelson, a front of house manager and stationery fiend who came to her *Only Connect* audition with her favourite book of Norfolk facts;
- Frederic Heath-Renn, a cryptic crossword enthusiast who has played ping pong in a salt mine and once saw a spoon used by Lenin;
- Eric Kilby, a statistician and keen genealogist who believes he has an IKEA bookcase named after him;

- Andy Crane, a retired business analyst who was once the caber-tossing champion of Birmingham;
- Josh Spero, a classics graduate who inadvertently ate a floral decoration at a parliamentary dinner;
- Margaret Gabica, a primary school teacher and keen linguist who once served an elephant in a supermarket;
- Ian Fellows, a vicar whose set of nativity scarecrows won the 2016 Wythenshawe Community Scarecrow Award;
- Tom West, a solicitor who recently spent the entire day on a train in order to attend a meeting at which only he was present;

and

- Richard Aubrey, a secondary school teacher and keen musician who's allergic to lions.

GAME 1

DIFFICULTY LEVEL: 1

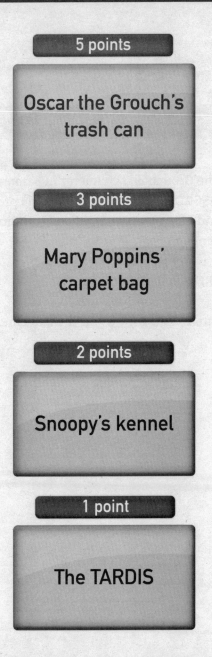

5 points

Oscar the Grouch's trash can

3 points

Mary Poppins' carpet bag

2 points

Snoopy's kennel

1 point

The TARDIS

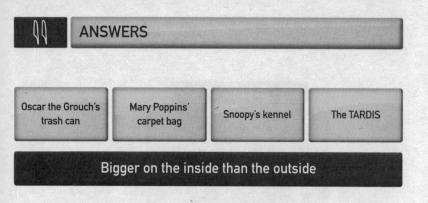

| Oscar the Grouch's trash can | Mary Poppins' carpet bag | Snoopy's kennel | The TARDIS |

Bigger on the inside than the outside

- Oscar the Grouch is a character in *Sesame Street*.
- In the 1964 Disney film, Mary Poppins produces a hat stand, mirror, plant and floor-standing lamp from her bag.
- Snoopy is in *Peanuts*.
- The TARDIS is in *Doctor Who*.

The Mountain Men got this on the last clue, for 1 point.

5 points

3 points

2 points

1 point

_____berry

These people's surnames can all be suffixed by 'berry' to give the name of a fruit

- Rabbi Lionel BLUE, who was a regular on Radio 4's *Thought for the Day*.
- Jack BLACK, actor and musician.
- Jack STRAW, former Home Secretary.
- Gabby LOGAN, former gymnast and presenter of sport on television.

No points for either the Orienteers (who went on to win series 10) or the Romantics.

5 points

Milan

3 points

Your party

2 points

My shirt

1 point

This song

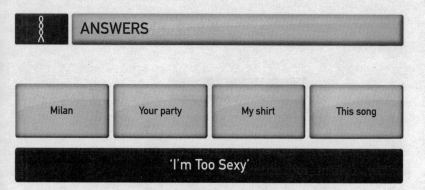

Milan | Your party | My shirt | This song

'I'm Too Sexy'

These are all things I'm too sexy for in the hit song by Right Said Fred, 'I'm Too Sexy'

- I'm too sexy for Milan, New York and Japan.
- I'm too sexy for your party, no way I'm disco dancing.
- I'm too sexy for my shirt, so sexy it hurts.
- I'm too sexy for this song (this is the last line of the song, naturally).

An impressive 3 points for the Scientists on this one.

It is sometimes baffling to the question editors when *Only Connect* is described as a 'highbrow' show ...

5 points

Seven consonants

3 points

Two vowels

2 points

Three syllables

1 point

Seven letters

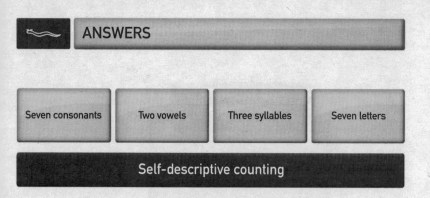
| Seven consonants | Two vowels | Three syllables | Seven letters |

Self-descriptive counting

- The word 'consonants' has 7 consonants.
- The word 'vowels' has 2 vowels.
- The word 'syllables' has 3 syllables.
- The word 'letters' has 7 letters in it.

Both the Road Trippers and the Builders drew a blank on this one.

5 points

Eurovision
Song Contest

3 points

Cow & Gate

2 points

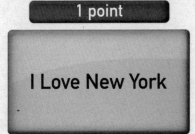

Wall's

1 point

I Love New York

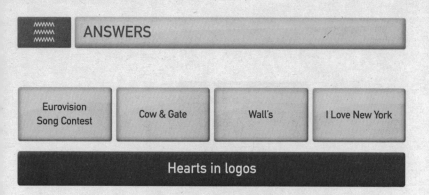

| Eurovision Song Contest | Cow & Gate | Wall's | I Love New York |

Hearts in logos

- The 'V' of the Eurovision Song Contest logo is a stylised heart.
- Cow & Gate is a company that produces formula milk for babies. Its logo is a red heart with the company's name in the middle.
- The ice cream company's logo is a swirling white heart on a red background.
- The slogan to promote tourism in New York has the word 'Love' replaced by a heart, and New York written as 'NY'.

The Cosmopolitans picked this up for 1 point as a bonus after the Taverners couldn't quite pin it down.

5 points

1/7 Iraq

3 points

2/7 Turkey

2 points

2/7 Egypt

1 point

2/7 Greece

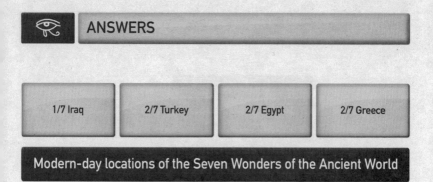
| 1/7 Iraq | 2/7 Turkey | 2/7 Egypt | 2/7 Greece |

Modern-day locations of the Seven Wonders of the Ancient World

- The Hanging Gardens of Babylon, thought to be in modern-day Iraq.
- The Temple of Artemis at Ephesus and the Mausoleum at Halicarnassus, both in modern-day Turkey.
- The Pharos or Lighthouse of Alexandria and the Great Pyramid of Giza, both in Egypt.
- The Statue of Zeus at Olympia and the Colossus of Rhodes, both in modern-day Greece.

Only the Great Pyramid of Giza, by far the oldest of the seven, survives today.

This question was picked by the Taverners, but they failed to spot the connection. Their opponents, the Bardophiles, nabbed a bonus point.

5 points

That place

3 points

This place

2 points

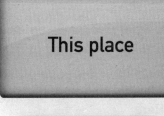

Before

?

| That place | This place | Before | (e.g.) Ancient Egyptian sun-god |

There, Here, Ere, Re

ACCEPT: anything that means 'Re', such as religious education, second musical note, rhenium, Royal Engineers, again, regarding, etc.

Remove the first letter from the word defined in one clue and you get the word defined in the next

- That place = There
- This place = Here
- Before = Ere
- Ancient Egyptian sun-god = Re (also known as Ra)

The Maltsters drew a blank on this one, and the Policy Wonks picked up a bonus point.

5 points

Base 9

3 points

Korf 8

2 points

Net 7

?

| Base 9 | Korf 8 | Net 7 | (e.g.) Volley 6 |

_____ball team sizes

ACCEPT: 6-a-side foot 6 (i.e. a football variant!)

- Baseball: 9-a-side.
- Korfball: 8-a-side. A sport invented in Holland (it means 'basket ball') with similarities to netball and basketball. Played internationally with mixed teams.
- Netball: 7-a-side, played throughout British Commonwealth countries.
- Volleyball: 6-a-side.

In this series 12 match, neither the Networkers nor the Cousins saw the sequence, so well done if you did at home.

5 points

Corrachadh Mòr

3 points

Dunnet Head

2 points

Lowestoft Ness

?

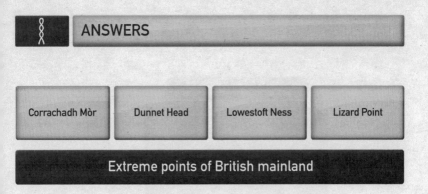

| Corrachadh Mòr | Dunnet Head | Lowestoft Ness | Lizard Point |

Extreme points of British mainland

DON'T ACCEPT: Land's End or anything offshore, e.g. the Channel Islands

These are the four extreme points of the British mainland, going clockwise from westernmost to southernmost

- Corrachadh Mòr in Highland, Scotland, is the westernmost.
- Dunnet Head in Caithness, Scotland, is the northernmost.
- Lowestoft Ness in Suffolk, England, now known officially as Ness Point, is the easternmost.
- Lizard Point in Cornwall, England, is the southernmost.

The Bookworms spotted this early, and picked it up for 3 points in their series 11 match against the Wayfarers.

5 points

arMs

3 points

hEart

2 points

neVus

?

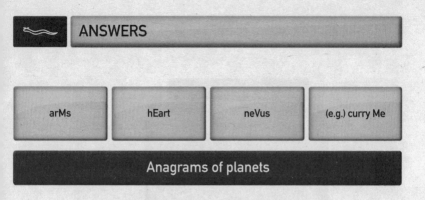

| arMs | hEart | neVus | (e.g.) curry Me |

Anagrams of planets

ACCEPT: any anagram of Mercury

- arMs = Mars
- hEart = Earth
- neVus = Venus (nevus is the American spelling of naevus, a congenital pigmented area on the skin)
- curry Me = Mercury

The Linguists solved this on Clue 2 to score 3 points in their match against the Oxonians.

5 points

Elder daughter
improvises music

3 points

Mother and
younger daughter
visit supermarket

2 points

Father leaves
power plant

?

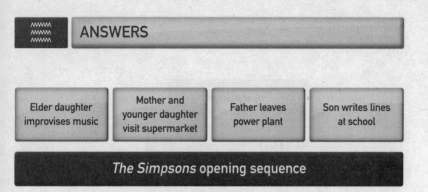

| Elder daughter improvises music | Mother and younger daughter visit supermarket | Father leaves power plant | Son writes lines at school |

The Simpsons opening sequence

This is the reverse order in which we meet the Simpsons in the programme's standard opening sequence

- Lisa improvises on saxophone during the school orchestra recital.
- Marge and Maggie are at the supermarket, with Maggie being put through the checkout.
- Homer leaves the power plant, with a stick of uranium stuck to his back.
- Bart writes lines on the school blackboard (albeit different lines each episode).

The Simpsons opening sequence has been redesigned twice in the show's history: once after the first season and once in 2009 to include more characters.

The Psmiths scored 2 points on this question, in their match against future series 12 champions the Verbivores.

5 points

3 points

2 points

?

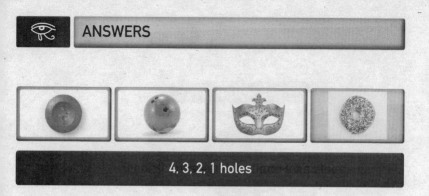

4, 3, 2, 1 holes

ACCEPT: anything with one hole (Polo mint, lifebelt)

Each clue has one less hole than the previous clue

- A button – this is a four-hole variety.
- A bowling ball – with holes for two fingers and a thumb.
- A mask – this is a Venetian mask with two holes for the eyes.
- A doughnut – a frosted ring doughnut.

In Series 8, the Bakers spotted this 'hidden in plain sight' sequence for 3 points in their match against the Press Gang.

Stuck	Gough	Crown	Clancy
Oxford	Percy	Chambers	Halfpenny
Florin	Macquarie	Male chauvinist	Judd
Farthing	Webster's	Collins	Guinea

CLUE WORDS

In the same group: Stuck and Percy

In the same group: Gough and Judd

Not in the same group: Chambers and Collins

Not in the same group: Guinea and Farthing

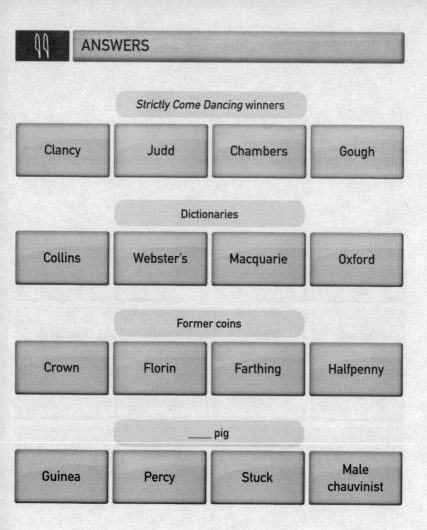

Strictly Come Dancing winners

| Clancy | Judd | Chambers | Gough |

Dictionaries

| Collins | Webster's | Macquarie | Oxford |

Former coins

| Crown | Florin | Farthing | Halfpenny |

_____ pig

| Guinea | Percy | Stuck | Male chauvinist |

The Wandering Minstrels scored 7 points on this wall.

Countdown	Lady Godiva	Opium	Fantasy
Perfection	Bob	Shalimar	Pointless
Tanner	15 to 1	No 5	Score
J'Adore	Bag of sand	Frontier	The Chase

CLUE WORDS

In the same group: Score and Frontier

In the same group: Tanner and Bag of sand

Not in the same group: Lady Godiva and No 5

Not in the same group: Countdown and The Chase

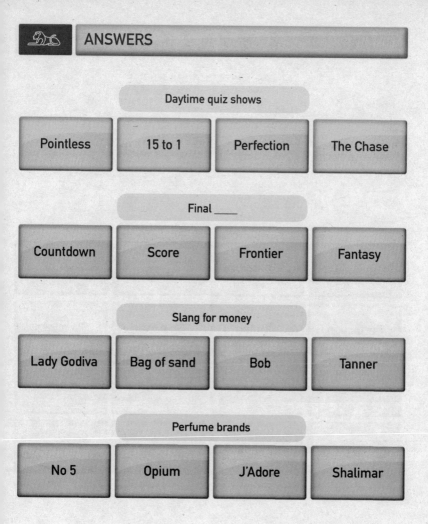

Daytime quiz shows

| Pointless | 15 to 1 | Perfection | The Chase |

Final ____

| Countdown | Score | Frontier | Fantasy |

Slang for money

| Lady Godiva | Bag of sand | Bob | Tanner |

Perfume brands

| No 5 | Opium | J'Adore | Shalimar |

The Cluesmiths solved this for the full 10 points.

Animals and their noises

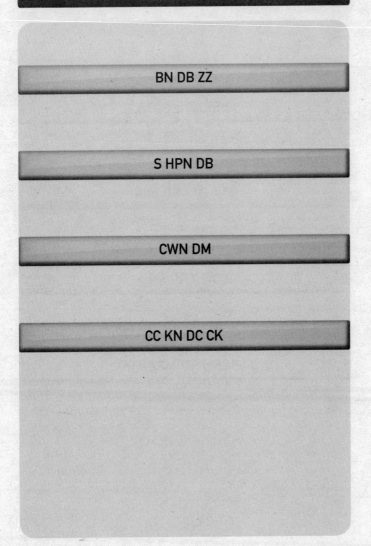

BN DB ZZ

S HPN DB

CWN DM

CC KN DC CK

Animals and their noises

BN DB ZZ

BEE AND BUZZ

S HPN DB

SHEEP AND BAA

CWN DM

COW AND MOO

CC KN DC CK

CUCKOO AND CUCKOO

Films set on Greek islands

Z RBT HG RK

MMMM

T HGN SFN V RN

S HR LYV LN TN

Films set on Greek islands

Z RBT HG RK

ZORBA THE GREEK

MMMM

MAMMA MIA!

T HGN SFN V RN

THE GUNS OF NAVARONE

S HR LYV LN TN

SHIRLEY VALENTINE

Things people say when shaking hands

H WD YD

PLS DT MT Y

WL LPL YD

C NG RTL TNS

Things people say when shaking hands

H WD YD

HOW DO YOU DO?

PLS DT MT Y

PLEASED TO MEET YOU

WL LPL YD

WELL PLAYED

C NG RTL TNS

CONGRATULATIONS

There are 50 …

W YSTL VYRL VR

MR CNS TTS

PN TSF RTHB LLS YNDR TS

S HD SFG RY

There are 50 ...

W YSTL VYRL VR

WAYS TO LEAVE YOUR LOVER

MR CNS TTS

AMERICAN STATES

PN TSF RTHB LLS YNDR TS

POINTS FOR THE BULLSEYE IN DARTS

S HD SFG RY

SHADES OF GREY

David Baddiel

5 points	3 points	2 points	
Piers Morgan	Phil Hall	Rebekah Wade	?

'I remember saying "Are they all terrible people?" to this. I also remember it being a moment I felt a little uncertain about afterwards – in that I do actually know both Rebekah Wade and Piers Morgan, and like all actual humans with the exception of George Galloway, they are complex personalities with both good and bad elements, and thus the joke was, I knew even as I was saying it, unfair to them and a reduction of the truth. However, I also knew it would get a laugh. Not only that, after it got a laugh, quite a big one, I didn't say to anyone at *Only Connect*, "Can we cut that, it's not really fair to Rebekah and Piers and I don't even know who Phil Hall is?", as I knew it would also get a laugh from people watching at home. Herein lies the splinter of ice at the heart of the comedian.'

Andy Coulson. (*News of the World* editors)

5 points

Pope John XX

3 points

The Traveling
Wilburys Vol. 2

2 points

Australian Open
1986

1 point

3–13 September
1752

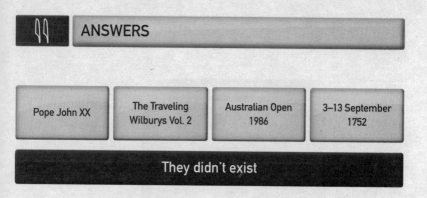

| Pope John XX | The Traveling Wilburys Vol. 2 | Australian Open 1986 | 3–13 September 1752 |

They didn't exist

None of these things existed, although they were preceded by, and followed by things that did exist

- Due to confusion in the medieval listing of popes named John, the twentieth Pope John (including antipopes) called himself John XXI instead of John XX.
- There was a Volume 1 and 3, but no Volume 2 from the Traveling Wilburys supergroup, which included Bob Dylan, Jeff Lynne, George Harrison, Tom Petty and Roy Orbison.
- The Australian Open was moved from December 1986 to January 1987, meaning there was no Open in 1986.
- In 1752, when the UK and its colonies changed from the Julian Calendar to the Gregorian calendar, there was no 3rd to 13th September (inclusive).

In a series 10 match against the History Boys, the Oxonians solved this on Clue 4.

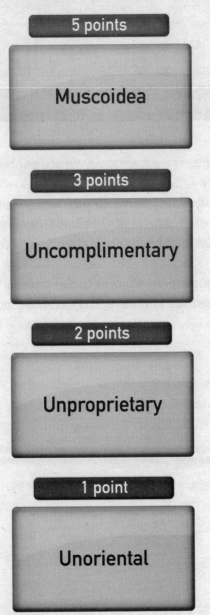

5 points

Muscoidea

3 points

Uncomplimentary

2 points

Unproprietary

1 point

Unoriental

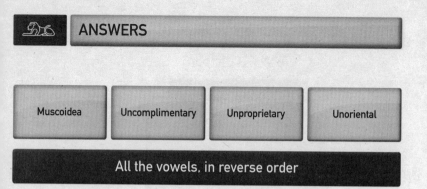

| Muscoidea | Uncomplimentary | Unproprietary | Unoriental |

All the vowels, in reverse order

- Muscoidea is a superfamily which contains the housefly.
- You would more normally say 'non-proprietary' and 'non-oriental', but that is intended to give a little clue here by drawing attention to the 'U's.

Another question that went to the Oxonians, this time against the Linguists. They scored 2 points.

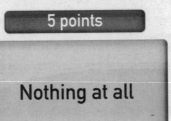
5 points

Nothing at all

3 points

Welsh psychedelic rock band

2 points

Superseded by FSA

1 point

Governing body of Scottish football

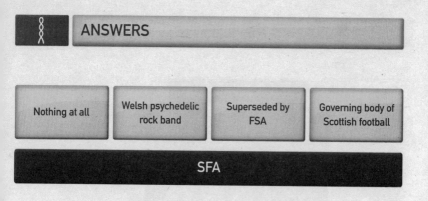

Nothing at all	Welsh psychedelic rock band	Superseded by FSA	Governing body of Scottish football

SFA

- Sweet Fanny Adams.
- Super Furry Animals.
- The Securities and Futures Authority (SFA) was replaced by the Financial Services Authority (FSA), which itself has now been replaced by the Financial Conduct Authority (FCA) and the Prudential Regulation Authority (PRA).
- Scottish Football Association.

This question fell to the QI Elves, who picked up 2 points.

5 points

The Pontipines
and the Wottingers

3 points

Miss Rachel
Haverford and
Atticus Finch

2 points

Prime Minister
and Chancellor of
the Exchequer

1 point

Smokie and Alice,
for 24 years

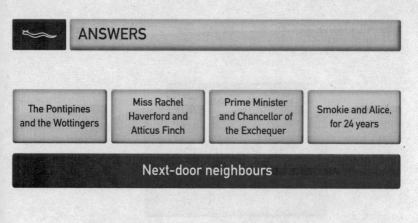

| The Pontipines and the Wottingers | Miss Rachel Haverford and Atticus Finch | Prime Minister and Chancellor of the Exchequer | Smokie and Alice, for 24 years |

Next-door neighbours

- The Pontipines and the Wottingers are families in *In the Night Garden*.
- Miss Rachel Haverford and Atticus Finch are characters in *To Kill a Mockingbird*.
- The Prime Minister and Chancellor of the Exchequer reside on Downing Street.
- Smokie had a hit with 'Living Next Door to Alice'. (Who on earth is Alice, anyway?)

Two points for the Genealogists in their series 12 showdown with the Wrestlers.

5 points

Malabo

3 points

Conakry

2 points

Port Moresby

1 point

Bissau

ANSWERS

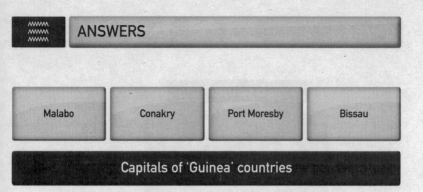

| Malabo | Conakry | Port Moresby | Bissau |

Capitals of 'Guinea' countries

- Malabo is the capital of Equatorial Guinea.
- Conakry is the capital of Guinea.
- Port Moresby is the capital of Papua New Guinea.
- Bissau is the capital of Guinea-Bissau.

The Tubers swallowed this up for 3 points against the Cosmopolitans, though it was not enough to stop them losing an epic battle by a single point.

5 points

3 points

2 points

1 point

London skyscrapers

These are nicknames (or actual names) of London skyscrapers

- The 'Cheesegrater' is the Leadenhall Building: public spaces opened in October 2014.
- The 'Walkie-Talkie' is 20 Fenchurch Street. In 2013 the Walkie-Talkie building was reported to have melted parked cars by focusing the sun's rays.
- The Shard is the tallest building in London. The Shard is, of course, its actual name.
- The 'Gherkin' is 30 St Mary Axe (previously the Swiss Re Building), designed by Norman Foster.

One point on this question for the Athenians against the Bookworms.

If you have an exceptional memory, you might recall that this question is slightly different from when it was broadcast in series 11. Clue 1 showed a helter-skelter, for the building at 22 Bishopsgate which was then under construction. Since then, its design has been changed, and it no longer looks like a helter-skelter, so we've updated the question!

5 points

A talking ...

3 points

To rub ...

2 points

The bee's ...

?

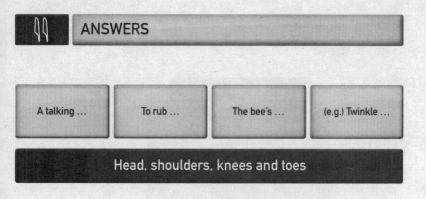

Head, shoulders, knees and toes

ACCEPT: any idiom ending with 'toes'

- 'A talking head' is someone talking on TV shown only from shoulders up.
- 'To rub shoulders' is to mix with others in some kind of social scenario.
- 'The bee's knees' is an excellent or ideally suitable person or thing (pre-twentieth century, it meant something small or insignificant).
- 'Twinkle toes' is used to describe someone who is sprightly.

This question appeared in the 2016 Sport Relief special. The BBC (Hugh Dennis, Julian Lloyd Webber and Lynne Truss) spotted it for 2 points.

5 points

Potomac: 1

3 points

Congo: 2

2 points

Nile: 3

?

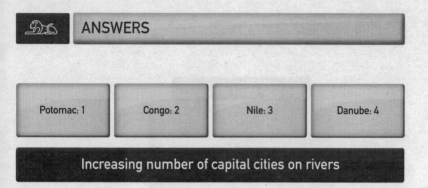

| Potomac: 1 | Congo: 2 | Nile: 3 | Danube: 4 |

Increasing number of capital cities on rivers

- Potomac: Washington, DC (USA).
- Congo: Kinshasa (DR Congo); Brazzaville (Congo).
- Nile: Juba (South Sudan) is on the White Nile; Khartoum (Sudan) is where the White Nile joins the Blue Nile to become the Nile; Cairo (Egypt) is on the Nile.
- Danube: Belgrade (Serbia); Budapest (Hungary); Bratislava (Slovakia); Vienna (Austria). The Danube is the only river with four capital cities on it.

The Psmiths failed to answer this correctly. Their opponents, the Verbivores, picked up a bonus. It's one of those questions that not only needs you to work out the sequence but also needs you to have the precise knowledge of what the answer will be.

5 points

Constituency MP:
Shaun Woodward

3 points

Shadow
Education:
Tim Collins

2 points

Opposition leader:
Michael Howard

?

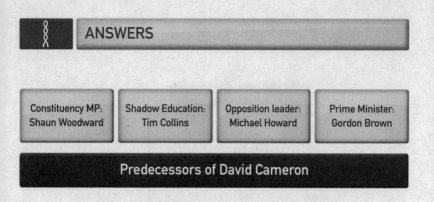

| Constituency MP: Shaun Woodward | Shadow Education: Tim Collins | Opposition leader: Michael Howard | Prime Minister: Gordon Brown |

Predecessors of David Cameron

- Cameron won Witney in 2001 when Woodward stood down after defecting from Conservative to Labour.
- Cameron became Shadow Secretary of State for Education and Skills in May 2005 when Collins lost his seat.
- Cameron was elected Conservative leader and Howard stood down in December 2005.
- Cameron took over from Brown as PM in May 2010.

This was in a Red Nose Day special. The Water Babies (Reeta Chakrabarti, Patrick Marber, Tom Holland) and the Tillers (Katie Derham, Steve Jones, Steve Pemberton) both missed it. Did you do any better?

5 points

N12

3 points

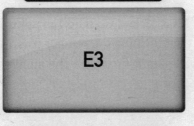

E3

2 points

S6

?

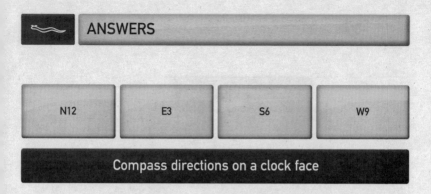

| N12 | E3 | S6 | W9 |

Compass directions on a clock face

These are the compass directions as superimposed on a clock face, going clockwise

The Oscar Men picked up a bonus point from the Maltsters. One of those incredibly frustrating/joyful *Only Connect* questions where the answer is staring you in the face.

5 points

Counter-intelligence

3 points

Terrorism

2 points

Revenge

?

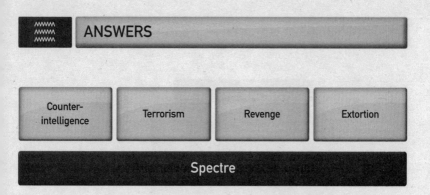

| Counter-intelligence | Terrorism | Revenge | Extortion |

Spectre

Spectre, from the James Bond films, is the Special Executive for Counter-intelligence, Terrorism, Revenge and Extortion

The first novel to mention Spectre was *Thunderball* in 1961, the first film was *Dr No* in 1962, and *Spectre* was the title of the twenty-fourth official Bond film from 2015.

In a series 12 match-up, the Part-Time Poets failed to spot it, allowing the Oscar Men to pick up a bonus point.

5 points

3 points

2 points

?

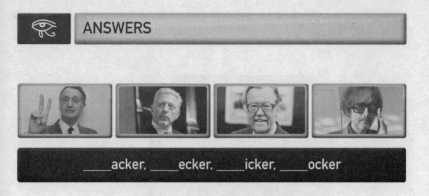

_____acker, _____ecker, _____icker, _____ocker

ACCEPT: anything ending in _____ocker

- Rt Hon. Jim Hacker – hapless minister played by Paul Eddington in *Yes Minister* and *Yes, Prime Minister*.
- Boris Becker – tennis player/commentator.
- Alan Whicker – journalist and broadcaster.
- Jarvis Cocker – Pulp singer.

The Athenians worked this out on Clue 3 in their match against the Scientists.

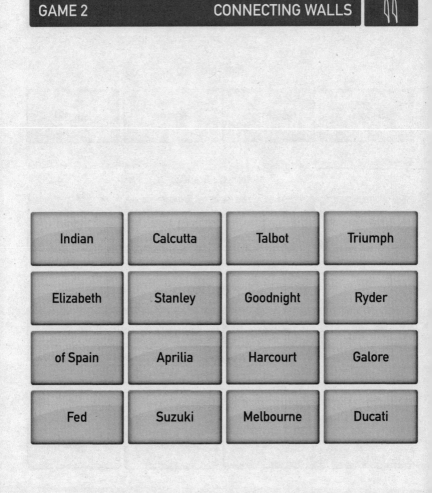

Indian	Calcutta	Talbot	Triumph
Elizabeth	Stanley	Goodnight	Ryder
of Spain	Aprilia	Harcourt	Galore
Fed	Suzuki	Melbourne	Ducati

CLUE WORDS

In the same group: Galore and Goodnight

In the same group: of Spain and Harcourt

Not in the same group: Suzuki and Ducati

Not in the same group: Ryder and Calcutta

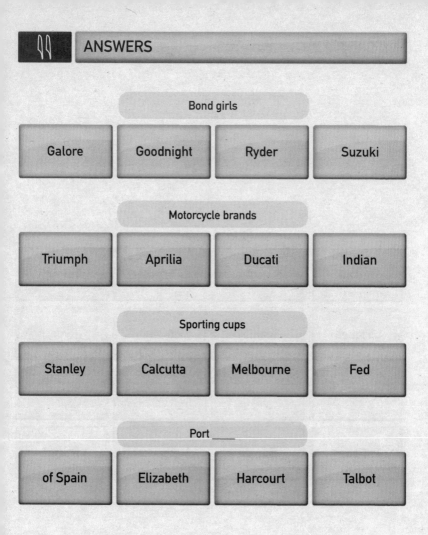

Bond girls

| Galore | Goodnight | Ryder | Suzuki |

Motorcycle brands

| Triumph | Aprilia | Ducati | Indian |

Sporting cups

| Stanley | Calcutta | Melbourne | Fed |

Port ____

| of Spain | Elizabeth | Harcourt | Talbot |

The Beekeepers scored 6 points on this wall.

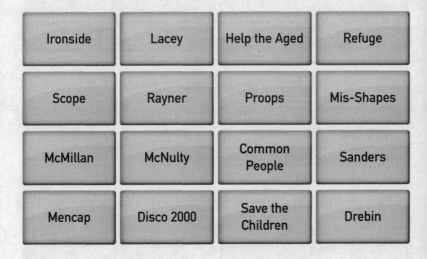

Ironside	Lacey	Help the Aged	Refuge
McMillan	McNulty	Common People	Sanders
Scope	Rayner	Proops	Mis-Shapes
Mencap	Disco 2000	Save the Children	Drebin

75

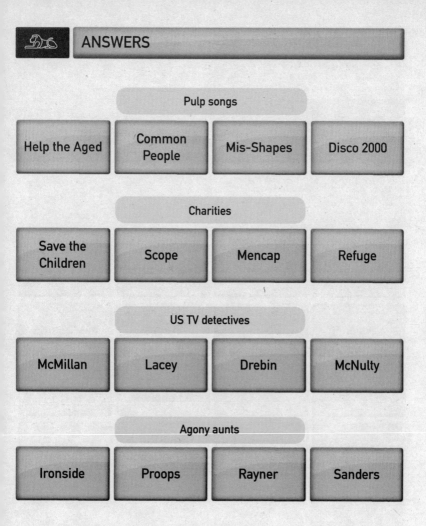

Pulp songs

| Help the Aged | Common People | Mis-Shapes | Disco 2000 |

Charities

| Save the Children | Scope | Mencap | Refuge |

US TV detectives

| McMillan | Lacey | Drebin | McNulty |

Agony aunts

| Ironside | Proops | Rayner | Sanders |

The Felinophiles scored a maximum 10 on this wall.

Moons

P HB S

KT HM N

R P

S NM YN GM N

Moons

P HB S

PHOBOS

KT HM N

KEITH MOON

R P

EUROPA

S NM YN GM N

SUN MYUNG MOON

Suns

THS NNSN DY

S NM CRSY ST MS

S NT Z

SN MYN GMN

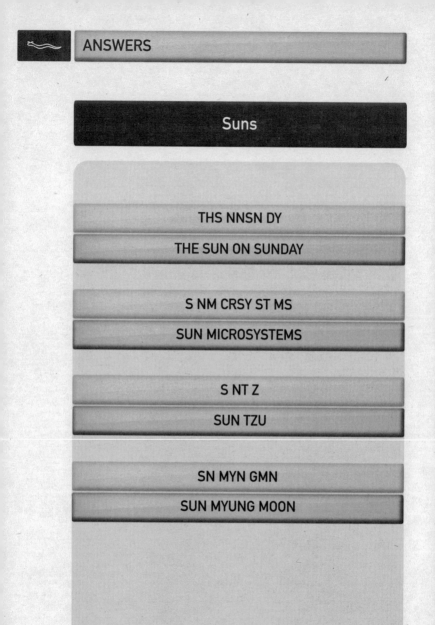

Suns

THS NNSN DY

THE SUN ON SUNDAY

S NM CRSY ST MS

SUN MICROSYSTEMS

S NT Z

SUN TZU

SN MYN GMN

SUN MYUNG MOON

Countries that start and end with the same letter

CNT RLF RC NRP BLC

R M N

NT GN DBR BD

SLM NSLN DS

Countries that start and end with the same letter

CNT RLF RC NRP BLC

CENTRAL AFRICAN REPUBLIC

R M N

ARMENIA

NT GN DBR BD

ANTIGUA AND BARBUDA

SLM NSLN DS

SOLOMON ISLANDS

'A few X short of a Y'

CR DSS HRTFD CK

CL W NSSH RTFC RCS

B RC KSS HR TFLD

S ND WC HSS HR TFPC NC

'A few X short of a Y'

CR DSS HRTFD CK

CARDS SHORT OF A DECK

CL W NSSH RTFC RCS

CLOWNS SHORT OF A CIRCUS

B RC KSS HR TFLD

BRICKS SHORT OF A LOAD

S ND WC HSS HR TFPC NC

SANDWICHES SHORT OF A PICNIC

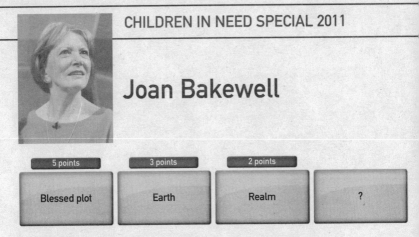

Joan Bakewell

5 points	3 points	2 points	
Blessed plot	Earth	Realm	?

'Quizzes fill me with dread ... this one above all.
But, hey, what's to lose when you're in your eighties?
I know nothing about pop culture – my time ends
with the Beatles and Bob Dylan. I know nothing about
sport, though I did once see Don Bradman play at Old
Trafford. I am not so much out of date as in another
time warp. But quotations ... I could be in with a
chance. At school in the forties we learnt great swathes
of poetry by heart. The odd thing about memory is that
it recalls stuff from when you were ten, but doesn't
remember last year's holidays. So, "Blessed plot" ...
I'm onto it like a ferret. Shakespeare's John of Gaunt
speech! And I knew what came fourth. But during the
chat afterwards ... which play? There was lots of gung-
ho patriotism around at the time. I guessed *Henry* V.
Wrong! It's *Richard II*. Getting that wrong stopped me
being too smug. But I am now.'

England. (John of Gaunt's monologue in *Richard II*)

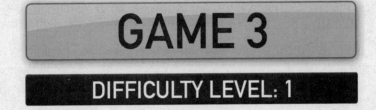

GAME 3

DIFFICULTY LEVEL: 1

5 points

Speedway:
Pedersen

3 points

Squash: Khan

2 points

Snooker: Higgins

1 point

F1 motor racing:
Hill

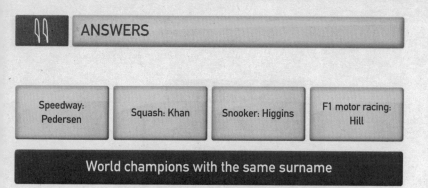

| Speedway: Pedersen | Squash: Khan | Snooker: Higgins | F1 motor racing: Hill |

World champions with the same surname

- Jan and Nicki Pedersen (both Denmark).
- Jahangir and Jansher Khan (both Pakistan).
- Alex and John Higgins (Northern Ireland and Scotland respectively).
- Phil Hill (USA); Graham and Damon Hill (England).

All unrelated except Graham and Damon Hill (father and son).

In a series 10 match the Chessmen picked up a point on this in their match against the Gallifreyans.

5 points

Pink Pinky

3 points

Orange Clyde

2 points

Red Blinky

1 point

Cyan Inky

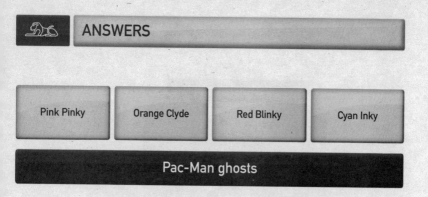

| Pink Pinky | Orange Clyde | Red Blinky | Cyan Inky |

Pac-Man ghosts

These are the colours and names of the ghosts in the game *Pac-Man*

- Pinky moves to four spaces ahead of Pac-Man.
- Clyde will chase Pac-Man if more than eight spaces away but otherwise moves to the bottom left corner.
- Blinky chases Pac-Man in Chase Mode and then returns to the maze corner.
- Inky moves to just in front of Pac-Man but its position is also determined by that of Blinky.

The Part-Time Poets scored 2 points on this in their game against the Surrealists.

5 points

Ungrammatical string follows

3 points

Multiply

2 points

Not out

1 point

Required field

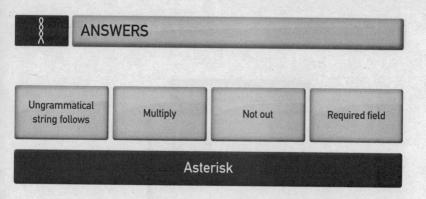

| Ungrammatical string follows | Multiply | Not out | Required field |

Asterisk

- In linguistics, an asterisk is used to indicate that what follows is not grammatically correct in the native language.
- In spreadsheet programs such as Excel, an asterisk is used as a multiplication sign.
- In cricket, an asterisk means 'Not out'.
- On online forms, an asterisk is used to indicate a field that you are required to fill in.

The Scunthorpe Scholars failed to spot this, and their opponents the Beekeepers picked up a bonus point.

5 points

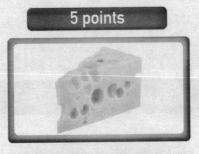

3 points

2 points

1 point

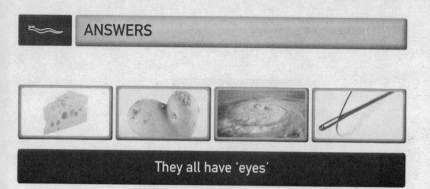

They all have 'eyes'

- The holes in Swiss cheese are called eyes.
- The nasty little buds on potatoes are called eyes.
- A small area of low pressure and calm in the centre of a tornado or cyclone is an eye.
- The hole at the end of a needle is an eye.

The Korfballers picked up 2 points on this question in a series 12 contest.

5 points

AUGUST 7

3 points

APOLLO 8

2 points

EXODUS 14

1 point

QUIZ 22

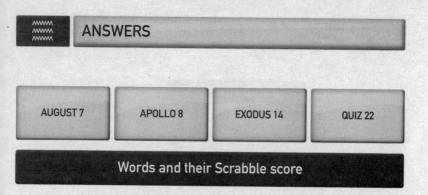

| AUGUST 7 | APOLLO 8 | EXODUS 14 | QUIZ 22 |

Words and their Scrabble score

- AUGUST: 1+1+2+1+1+1 = 7
- APOLLO: 1+3+1+1+1+1 = 8
- EXODUS: 1+8+1+2+1+1 = 14
- QUIZ: 10+1+1+10 = 22

The Korfballers scored a point on this question against the Shutterbugs.

One thing it is always worth asking is why a clue is not laid out in the normal way. The clues being in capitals can be a pointer to the question being a word puzzle.

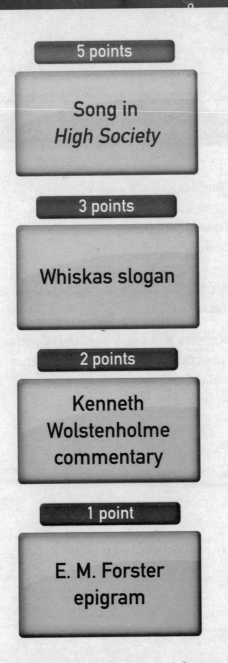

5 points

Song in *High Society*

3 points

Whiskas slogan

2 points

Kenneth Wolstenholme commentary

1 point

E. M. Forster epigram

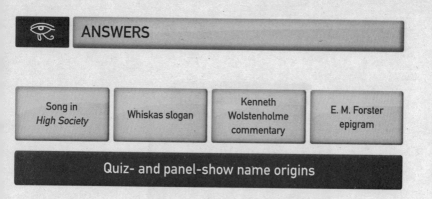
| Song in *High Society* | Whiskas slogan | Kenneth Wolstenholme commentary | E. M. Forster epigram |

Quiz- and panel-show name origins

- Who Wants to Be a Millionaire?
- 8 Out of 10 Cats
- They Think It's All Over
- Only Connect

Two points for the Wayfarers against the Bookworms.

Regular viewers will know that *Only Connect* lends itself to the odd self-referential question.

5 points

1 (2)

3 points

2 (3,5)

2 points

3 (7,11,13)

?

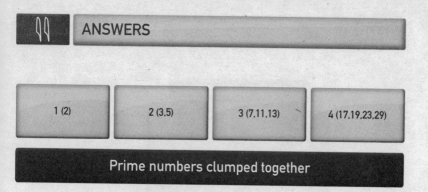

| 1 (2) | 2 (3,5) | 3 (7,11,13) | 4 (17,19,23,29) |

Prime numbers clumped together

- The first prime number is 2.
- The next two prime numbers are 3 and 5.
- The next three are 7, 11 and 13.
- The next four are 17, 19, 23 and 29.

The Verbivores proved they could do numbers as well as words by scoring 2 points on this question in their match against the Psmiths.

5 points

1st: Chelsea

3 points

1st: Barbara

2 points

1st: Malia

?

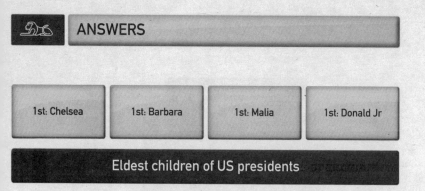

| 1st: Chelsea | 1st: Barbara | 1st: Malia | 1st: Donald Jr |

Eldest children of US presidents

ACCEPT: Ivanka, if the reasoning is "eldest daughter" otherwise DO NOT ACCEPT: Eric, Ivanka, Tiffany or Barron if the reasoning is "eldest child"

- Chelsea Clinton, daughter of Bill and Hillary Clinton, is an only child.
- Barbara Bush, daughter of George W. and Laura Bush, is the elder of twins.
- Malia, daughter of Barack and Michelle Obama, is the elder of two.
- Donald Jr, first child of Donald and Ivana Trump. He is the oldest of five siblings and half-siblings.

In a series 9 match, the Software Engineers spotted this for 3 points in their match against the Welsh Learners.

The question has changed since broadcast in 2014 (where it started with George and ended with Malia). It might have been expected, at that point, that the answer would be Chelsea again ...

5 points

3 points

2 points

?

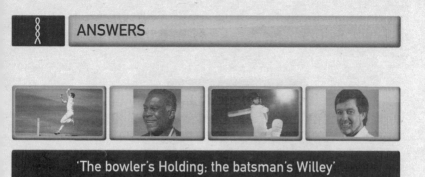

'The bowler's Holding; the batsman's Willey'

This depicts Brian Johnston's legendary piece of cricket commentary, apparently said at the Oval in 1976, when the West Indies' Michael Holding bowled to England's Peter Willey. Johnners read out a letter alleging that he had said it, but there is no recorded evidence that he did. *Test Match Special* boss Peter Baxter has said that the seemingly mischievous letter was sent by 'a Miss Tess Tickle'.

In series 11, the Polyglots failed to answer this, and their opponents the Yorkers, in keeping with their name, snapped it up for a bonus point.

5 points

Poisoned

3 points

Stabbed by
Prince Ludwig

2 points

Becomes
Prince Regent

?

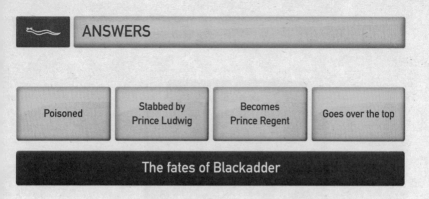

| Poisoned | Stabbed by Prince Ludwig | Becomes Prince Regent | Goes over the top |

The fates of Blackadder

ACCEPT: 'Going into battle', etc

- Series 1 – The court of 'Richard IV'. Prince Edmund accidentally poisons himself in a plot to steal the throne.
- Series 2 – The court of Elizabeth I. Prince Ludwig kills the entire cast while disguised as the queen.
- Series 3 – The court of Prince George, the Prince Regent. Swaps identities with the Prince, who is then killed in a duel with the Duke of Wellington. Edmund assumes the identity of the Prince.
- Series 4 – World War I trenches. The viewer assumes he is mowed down by machine-gun fire while going over the top (we do not see him die, only running in slow motion across no-man's-land with his comrades).

The Romantics scored 2 points on this in their series 10 match against the Orienteers.

5 points

Mastercard

3 points

Rubik's Magic

2 points

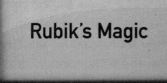

Audi

?

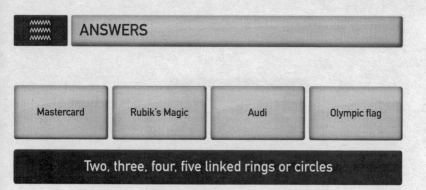

| Mastercard | Rubik's Magic | Audi | Olympic flag |

Two, three, four, five linked rings or circles

ACCEPT: anything with five rings

- The Mastercard logo is two interlinked rings.
- Rubik's Magic was a Rubik puzzle consisting of eight double-sided plastic panels which were hinged together with wires. In its shop-bought or solved state, the puzzle shows three interlinked rings.
- Audi's logo is four linked rings.
- The Olympic flag is five linked rings (blue, black, red, yellow, green) on a white background.

In series 6, the Educators spotted this on Clue 3 in their match against the Wordsmiths.

5 points

M

3 points

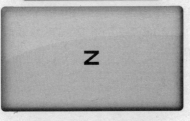

N

2 points

O

?

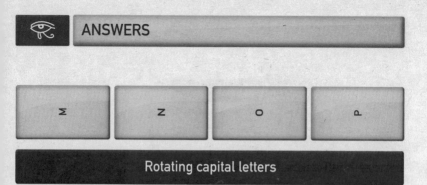

Rotating capital letters

How did you do on this? Well done if you did as well as the Verbivores, who took the risk and scored the maximum 5. Considering they ended up beating the Fire-Eaters by 4 points, it was a pretty decisive gamble.

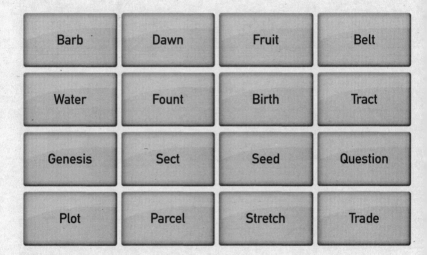

Barb	Dawn	Fruit	Belt
Water	Fount	Birth	Tract
Genesis	Sect	Seed	Question
Plot	Parcel	Stretch	Trade

CLUE WORDS

In the same group: Genesis and Fount

In the same group: Barb and Sect

Not in the same group: Tract and Plot

Not in the same group: Question and Stretch

Beginnings

| Dawn | Fount | Seed | Genesis |

Marks

| Question | Birth | Trade | Water |

Areas of land

| Plot | Belt | Parcel | Stretch |

____arian

| Tract | Fruit | Barb | Sect |

The Collectors scored 4 points on this wall.

Plane	Avocado	Bradawl	KenKen
Jigsaw	Tangram	Guava	Adze
Durian	Chisel	Monsoon	Crossword
Oasis	Tentaizu	Mango	Rambutan

CLUE WORDS

In the same group: KenKen and Crossword
In the same group: Bradawl and Chisel
Not in the same group: Mango and Guava
Not in the same group: Jigsaw and Tangram

115

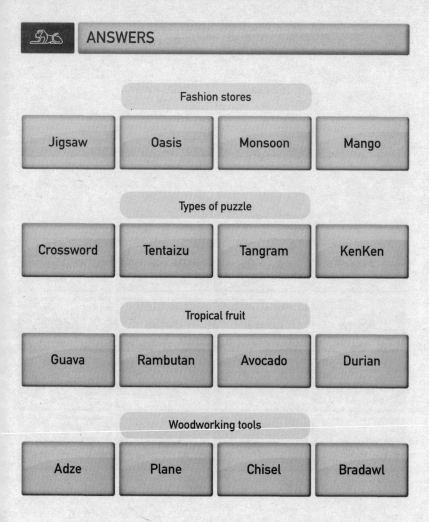

Fashion stores

Jigsaw	Oasis	Monsoon	Mango

Types of puzzle

Crossword	Tentaizu	Tangram	KenKen

Tropical fruit

Guava	Rambutan	Avocado	Durian

Woodworking tools

Adze	Plane	Chisel	Bradawl

The Oscar Men scored a maximum 10 on this wall, but still came second in the game to the Part-Time Poets, losing by just 1 point.

Sisters

VN SN D S RN

LS N DNN

B TR CND GN

CH RLT TM LYN DNN

Sisters

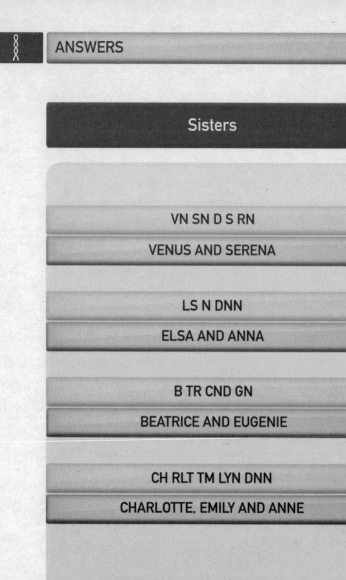

VN SN D S RN

VENUS AND SERENA

LS N DNN

ELSA AND ANNA

B TR CND GN

BEATRICE AND EUGENIE

CH RLT TM LYN DNN

CHARLOTTE, EMILY AND ANNE

- Venus and Serena Williams.
- Elsa and Anna from Disney's *Frozen*.
- Princesses Beatrice and Eugenie.
- Charlotte, Emily and Anne Brontë.

Six-syllable words

RS P NSB LTY

NCY CL PD

NM TP

PRP HR NL

Six-syllable words

RS P NSB LTY

RESPONSIBILITY

NCY CL PD

ENCYCLOPÆDIA

NM TP

ONOMATOPOEIA

PRP HR NL

PARAPHERNALIA

Often found on a curriculum vitae

W RK XPR NC

RF RN CS

DCTN NDQ LFC TNS

D DTN LSK LLS

Often found on a curriculum vitae

W RK XPR NC

WORK EXPERIENCE

RF RN CS

REFERENCES

DCTN NDQ LFC TNS

EDUCATION AND QUALIFICATIONS

D DTN LSK LLS

ADDITIONAL SKILLS

A chemical element and its symbol

L DN DP B

X YGNN D

RNN DF

D N N D

A chemical element and its symbol

L DN DP B

LEAD AND PB

X YGNN D

OXYGEN AND O

RNN DF

IRON AND FE

D N N D

IODINE AND I

Mark Gatiss

5 points	3 points	2 points	1 point
Speedy robber	Iguana tooth	Roof lizard	Three-horned face

'I did know it! We just didn't get it! It was on the tip of my brain. This is something I would have known when I was eight. I'm very ashamed. Then again, we did win the match.'

Literal names of dinosaurs

- Speedy robber: Velociraptor.
- Iguana tooth: Iguanodon.
- Roof lizard: Stegosaurus.
- Three-horned face: Triceratops.

GAME 4

DIFFICULTY LEVEL: 2

5 points

3 points

2 points

1 point

English city homophones

- (Derby) Rhys Darby: New Zealand comedian, Murray in *Flight of the Conchords*.
- (Ely) Jennifer Ehle: played Elizabeth Bennet in the BBC's *Pride and Prejudice*.
- (Ripon, one of the smallest cities in England) Angela Rippon: first woman to regularly present the national news on the BBC.
- (Leicester) Adrian Lester: star of *Hustle*.

The Highgates got this off the last clue in their match against the Shutterbugs.

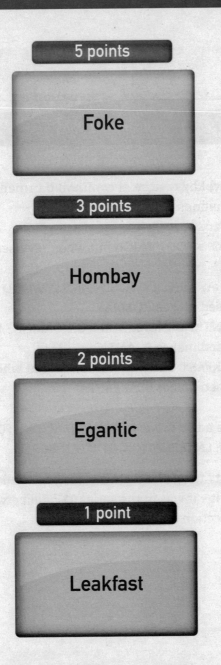

5 points

Foke

3 points

Hombay

2 points

Egantic

1 point

Leakfast

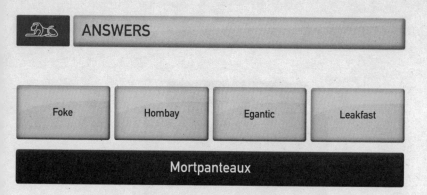
| Foke | Hombay | Egantic | Leakfast |

Mortpanteaux

These are the reverse of common portmanteaux (combinations of words)

- SMOKE + FOG = SMOG but when reversed makes FOKE.
- BOMBAY + HOLLYWOOD = BOLLYWOOD but when reversed makes HOMBAY.
- GIGANTIC + ENORMOUS = GINORMOUS but when reversed makes EGANTIC.
- BREAKFAST + LUNCH = BRUNCH but when reversed makes LEAKFAST.

Here are a few more: COMA (DRAMEDY), FOON (SPORK), ENTERCATION (EDUTAINMENT).

No points for either team on this one. Well done if you got it – it was in the series 11 final between the String Section and the Wayfarers.

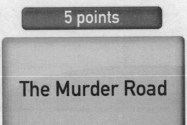

5 points

The Murder Road

3 points

Flaubert's Company

2 points

Where Convocations Dare

1 point

The Parliament and the Pussy-Cat

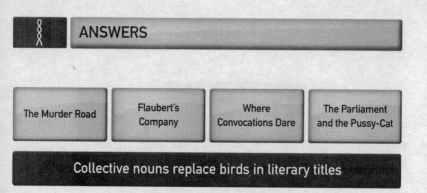

| The Murder Road | Flaubert's Company | Where Convocations Dare | The Parliament and the Pussy-Cat |

Collective nouns replace birds in literary titles

- *The Crow Road*, novel by Iain Banks (a murder of crows).
- *Flaubert's Parrot*, novel by Julian Barnes (a company of parrots).
- *Where Eagles Dare*, World War II adventure thriller by Alistair MacLean (a convocation of eagles).
- 'The Owl and the Pussy-Cat', poem by nonsense poet Edward Lear (a parliament of owls).

The Cosmopolitans scored 2 points on this question in their match against the Taverners.

5 points

Liam Gallagher (guitar): 'Roll With It'

3 points

A ventriloquist's dummy (vocals): 'Lonely This Christmas'

2 points

John Peel (mandolin): 'Maggie May'

1 point

Nobody (nothing): first 1:20 of 'Martha's Harbour'

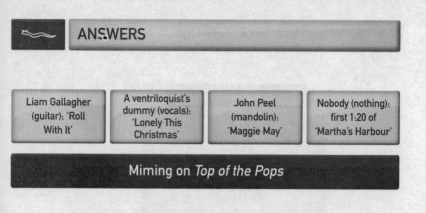

| Liam Gallagher (guitar): 'Roll With It' | A ventriloquist's dummy (vocals): 'Lonely This Christmas' | John Peel (mandolin): 'Maggie May' | Nobody (nothing): first 1:20 of 'Martha's Harbour' |

Miming on *Top of the Pops*

Each clue gives an artist, and what was unusually mimed during a song in an appearance on *Top of the Pops*

- 'Roll With It': for fun, Noel pretended to sing and Liam mimed playing guitar.
- 'Lonely This Christmas': Les Gray, on Mud's 1974 Christmas no. 1, explained that miming the singing parts was relatively easy, but miming to a spoken part was almost impossible, so he didn't bother.
- 'Maggie May': Rod Stewart asked Peel to come on and mime the mandolin part. It was actually played by Ray Jackson of the band Lindisfarne.
- 'Martha's Harbour': All About Eve appeared live and couldn't hear the foldback so sat doing nothing, unaware they were 'on'. A big cheer came from the crowd when the track eventually became audible, so the band at last began miming.

The Networkers failed to answer this, so it was picked up for a bonus by their opponents the Psmiths.

5 points

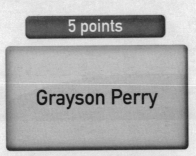

Grayson Perry

3 points

Sebastian Flyte

2 points

Spotty Man

1 point

Christopher Robin

| Grayson Perry | Sebastian Flyte | Spotty Man | Christopher Robin |

Friends with teddy bears

- Artist Grayson Perry's childhood bear is called Alan Measles.
- In *Brideshead Revisited*, Sebastian Flyte's constant companion is his teddy bear Aloysius.
- Spotty Man is best friends with SuperTed, in the cartoon *SuperTed* (Spotty Man does not actually own SuperTed, but it would be harsh to disallow 'teddy bear owners'). The executive producer of *Only Connect* wrote the theme tune for *SuperTed*.
- Christopher Robin is the best friend of Winnie-the-Pooh, in the books by A. A. Milne.

The Policy Wonks picked up a crucial 3 points on this question in their match against the Maltsters.

5 points

From its coastal capital city

3 points

From its highest mountain

2 points

From being established by freed slaves

1 point

From being a republic in the centre of Africa

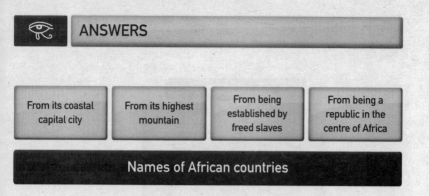

| From its coastal capital city | From its highest mountain | From being established by freed slaves | From being a republic in the centre of Africa |

Names of African countries

All of these clues describe where certain African countries got their name from

- Djibouti was named after its coastal capital city in 1977.
- Kenya is named after Mount Kenya.
- Liberia comes from the Latin '*liber*', meaning free.
- Central African Republic is named after its location.

The Oxonians picked this up as a bonus from the Politicos.

The last clue can be seen as a bit of a nod to a favourite answer on *Pointless*.

5 points

Seine

3 points

Setter

2 points

Ottoman

?

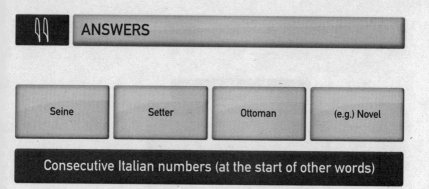

| Seine | Setter | Ottoman | (e.g.) Novel |

Consecutive Italian numbers (at the start of other words)

- *Sei* – Six
- *Sette* – Seven
- *Otto* – Eight
- *Nove* – Nine

In series 10, neither the Nightwatchmen nor the Nordiphiles spotted this, so well done if you did.

5 points

1994: Torvill & Dean – Olympic ice dance competition

3 points

1995: *Panorama* Special – Princess Diana

2 points

1996: *Only Fools and Horses* Christmas special part 3

?

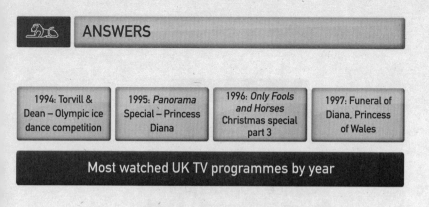

| 1994: Torvill & Dean – Olympic ice dance competition | 1995: *Panorama* Special – Princess Diana | 1996: *Only Fools and Horses* Christmas special part 3 | 1997: Funeral of Diana, Princess of Wales |

Most watched UK TV programmes by year

- 23.95 million.
- 22.78 million.
- 24.35 million: the Trotters finally become millionaires.
- 19.29 million.

An impressive 3 points for the Fire-Eaters in their match against the Korfballers.

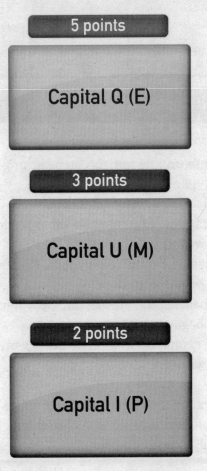

5 points

Capital Q (E)

3 points

Capital U (M)

2 points

Capital I (P)

?

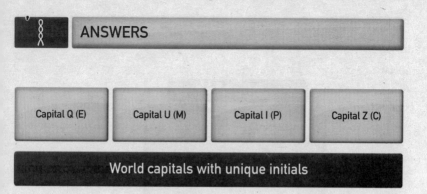

Capital Q (E)   Capital U (M)   Capital I (P)   Capital Z (C)

World capitals with unique initials

Oddly, these unique initials can be arranged to spell the word 'quiz'

- Quito, capital of Ecuador. No other world capital begins with Q.
- Ulaanbaatar, capital of Mongolia. No other world capital begins with U.
- Islamabad, capital of Pakistan. No other world capital begins with I.
- Zagreb, capital of Croatia. No other world capital begins with Z.

Two points for the Verbivores in the series 12 final against the Cosmopolitans. A classic quiz fact and a classic *Only Connect* question.

5 points

Start of 1929 Wall Street Crash

3 points

Sterling withdraws from ERM

2 points

Irish budget deficit reaches 32% of GDP

?

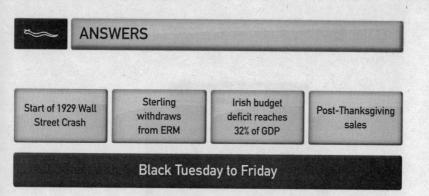

| Start of 1929 Wall Street Crash | Sterling withdraws from ERM | Irish budget deficit reaches 32% of GDP | Post-Thanksgiving sales |

Black Tuesday to Friday

ACCEPT: any other example meaning Black Friday, e.g. 'Day gold prices plummeted', or indeed just the words 'Black Friday'

- 29 Oct 1929: 16 million shares traded, taken to be the beginning of the Crash.
- 16 Sept 1992: Britain forced to leave European Exchange Rate Mechanism.
- 30 Sept 2010: announcement of cost of bailout of Anglo Irish Bank.
- Post-Thanksgiving sales: annual shopping frenzy.

One point against the head for the Mixologists versus the Collectors.

5 points

(e.g.) delta

3 points

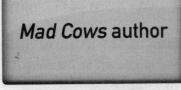

Mad Cows author

2 points

Native of Latvia

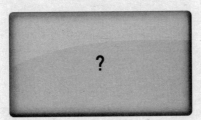

?

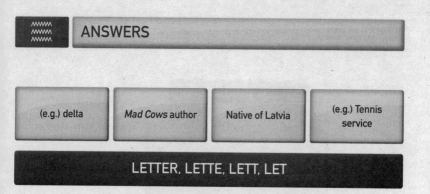

| (e.g.) delta | *Mad Cows* author | Native of Latvia | (e.g.) Tennis service |

LETTER, LETTE, LETT, LET

ACCEPT: rental property or other definitions of let

- Delta – LETTER: fourth letter of Greek alphabet.
- *Mad Cows* author – Kathy LETTE: Australian author.
- Native of Latvia – LETT: native or citizen of Latvia or area formerly known as Lettland.
- Tennis service – LET.

In series 9, the Erstwhile Athletes spotted this on Clue 3 in their match against the Software Engineers.

5 points

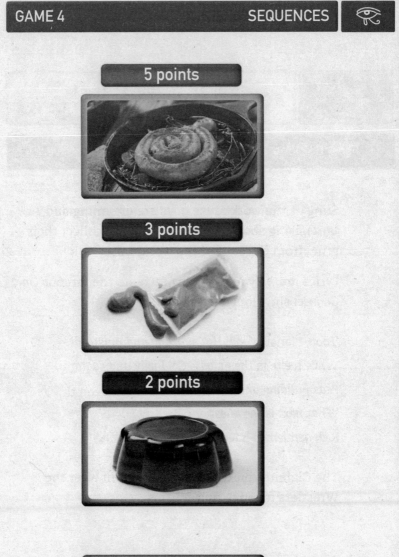

3 points

2 points

?

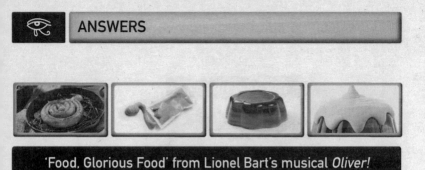

'Food, Glorious Food' from Lionel Bart's musical *Oliver!*

Sung as the workhouse boys are dreaming and fantasising about food while going to collect their gruel from the staff of the workhouse.

Lyrics are ... (you may now recreate the famous *Only Connect* singalong experience):

'Food, glorious food! Hot sausage and mustard!
While we're in the mood – Cold jelly and custard!
Peas pudding and saveloys,
What next is the question?
Rich gentlemen have it, boys – indigestion.'

The Clareites picked up a bonus point after the Wrestlers failed to answer this.

Picard	Kael	Bergamasco	Norman
Ebert	Lancashire Heeler	Bazin	Kirk
Schapendoes	Janeway	Provençal	Archer
Sisko	Collie	Kermode	Alsatian

CLUE WORDS
In the same group: Bazin and Kermode
In the same group: Lancashire Heeler and Schapendoes
Not in the same group: Picard and Kirk
Not in the same group: Alsatian and Collie

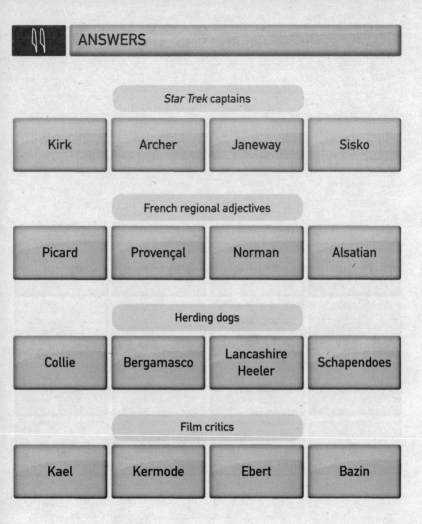

Star Trek captains

| Kirk | Archer | Janeway | Sisko |

French regional adjectives

| Picard | Provençal | Norman | Alsatian |

Herding dogs

| Collie | Bergamasco | Lancashire Heeler | Schapendoes |

Film critics

| Kael | Kermode | Ebert | Bazin |

An impressive 10 points on this wall for the Wayfarers.

Zodiac	House	Square	Seven
Pointer	Panic Room	Münsterländer	Ascendant
Scissor	Fight Club	Conjunction	Brittany
Italian spinone	Ugly	Gone Girl	Magdalene

CLUE WORDS

In the same group: Italian spinone and Münsterländer

In the same group: Panic Room and Fight Club

Not in the same group: Conjunction and Zodiac

Not in the same group: Pointer and Scissor

David Fincher films

Fight Club	Gone Girl	Panic Room	Zodiac

_____ Sisters

Magdalene	Scissor	Seven	Ugly

Astrological terms

Ascendant	Conjunction	House	Square

Gun dogs

Pointer	Brittany	Münsterländer	Italian spinone

Five points on this wall for the Builders.

Sayings without the 'and' in the middle

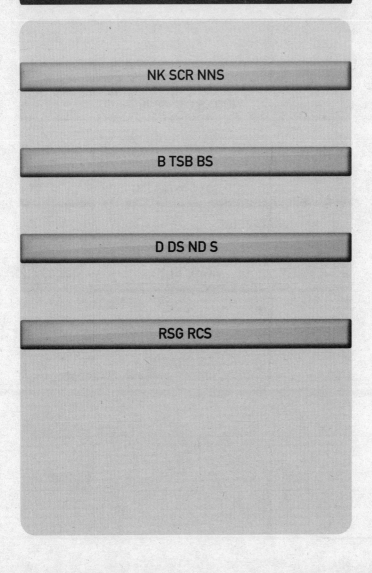

NK SCR NNS

B TSB BS

D DS ND S

RSG RCS

Sayings without the 'and' in the middle

NK SCR NNS

NOOKS CRANNIES

B TSB BS

BITS BOBS

D DS ND S

ODDS ENDS

RSG RCS

AIRS GRACES

Works of Salvador Dalí

THB RN NGG RFF

PPRT SND HND

T HPRS STN CFM MRY

LB ST RTLP HN

Works of Salvador Dalí

THB RN NGG RFF

THE BURNING GIRAFFE

PPRT SND HND

APPARATUS AND HAND

T HPRS STN CFM MRY

THE PERSISTENCE OF MEMORY

LB ST RTLP HN

LOBSTER TELEPHONE

Questions a waiter might ask

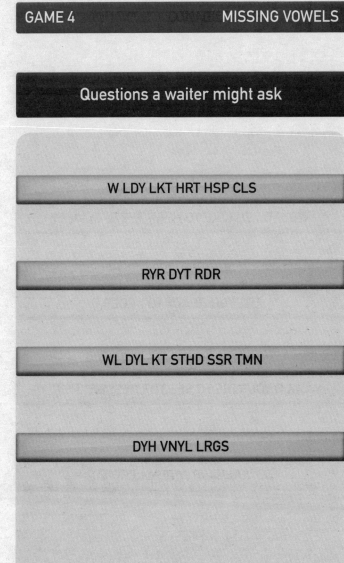

W LDY LKT HRT HSP CLS

RYR DYT RDR

WL DYL KT STHD SSR TMN

DYH VNYL RGS

Questions a waiter might ask

W LDY LKT HRT HSP CLS

WOULD YOU LIKE TO HEAR THE SPECIALS?

RYR DYT RDR

ARE YOU READY TO ORDER?

WL DYL KT STHD SSR TMN

WOULD YOU LIKE TO SEE THE DESSERT MENU?

DYH VNYL LRGS

DO YOU HAVE ANY ALLERGIES?

Films merged with US states

TH RSSM TH NG BTM RYL ND

THNG HTM RBF RCHR STM SSC HST TS

GNW THTH WNDN

RD RSF THL STRK NSS

163

Films merged with US states

TH RSSM TH NG BTM RYL ND

THERE'S SOMETHING ABOUT MARYLAND

THNG HTM RBF RCHR STM SSC HST TS

THE NIGHTMARE BEFORE CHRISTMASSACHUSETTS

GNW THTH WNDN

GONE WITH THE WINDIANA

RD RSF THL STRK NSS

RAIDERS OF THE LOST ARKANSAS

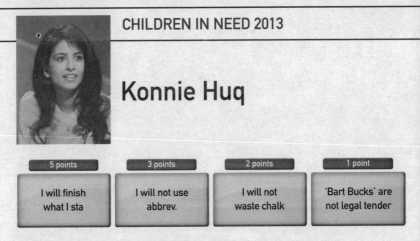

Konnie Huq

5 points	3 points	2 points	1 point
I will finish what I sta	I will not use abbrev.	I will not waste chalk	'Bart Bucks' are not legal tender

'I was pleased to get that right. It's weird because I remember going to a pub quiz once and there was a tie-breaker about *The Simpsons*, and I got that too. It was a bit fluky. I'd love to say my best area of expertise is astrophysics, but clearly it's *The Simpsons*.'

The Simpsons chalkboard gags

GAME 5

DIFFICULTY LEVEL: 2

5 points

**1
(Gaelic football)**

3 points

**1 or 3
(American football)**

2 points

**1 or 2
(Rugby league)**

1 point

**2 or 3
(Rugby union)**

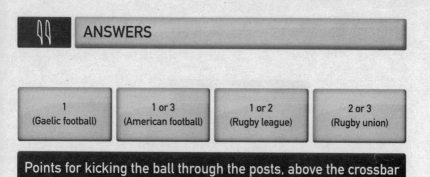

| 1 (Gaelic football) | 1 or 3 (American football) | 1 or 2 (Rugby league) | 2 or 3 (Rugby union) |

Points for kicking the ball through the posts, above the crossbar

- Gaelic football: 1 point for kicking (or punching) the ball between the posts, over the crossbar (it's 3 points for kicking/punching it below the crossbar, into the net).
- American football: 1 for an extra point, after a touchdown; 3 for a field goal.
- Rugby league: 1 point for a drop goal; 2 points for a conversion or a penalty.
- Rugby union: 2 points for a conversion; 3 for a penalty kick or a drop goal.

The question fell to the Part-Time Poets in series 12. They failed to spot it, however, and the Surrealists picked up a bonus point.

5 points

Tuvalu

3 points

Hijab

2 points

Defra

1 point

Nope

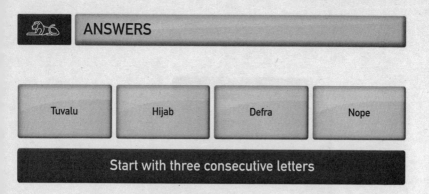

| Tuvalu | Hijab | Defra | Nope |

Start with three consecutive letters

- Country (T-U-V).
- Veil (H-I-J).
- Government department (D-E-F).
- Meaning 'no' (N-O-P).

The setter's original note on this was: 'I just liked that TUVALU is now in the quizzers' lexicon (from *Pointless* and the .tv domain name) so it wrongfoots you immediately.'

The Surrealists (and their opponents the Korfballers) failed to see what was staring them in the face.

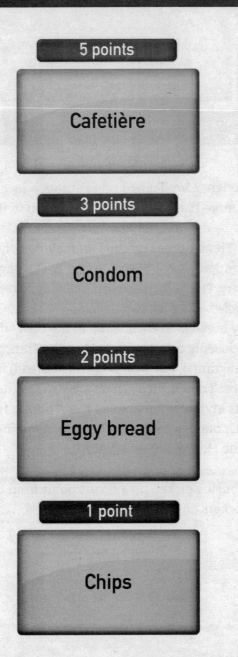

5 points

Cafetière

3 points

Condom

2 points

Eggy bread

1 point

Chips

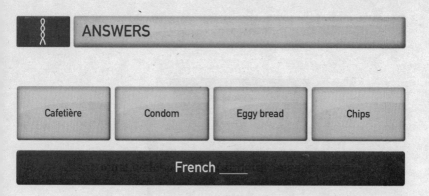

| Cafetière | Condom | Eggy bread | Chips |

French _____

- Cafetière AKA 'French press', though its origins are more likely Italian. Usage of term in the USA may be due to 1993 *New York Times* article about the 'French-press method' of making coffee.
- A condom was a 'French letter' to the English gentry. The French, in turn, called it '*la capote anglaise*' – English cap.
- Eggy bread is 'French toast' in the USA (after supposedly being brought there by French immigrants), but '*pain perdu*' (lost bread) in France.
- Chips: 'French fries'. There are various theories to its etymology, including that Thomas Jefferson had 'potatoes served in the French manner' at a White House dinner in 1802.

The Cousins picked up a bonus point from the Networkers on this question.

5 points

Actor who played the Joker on TV

3 points

Johannesburg football club

2 points

Ivan the Terrible, Peter the Great, etc.

1 point

Mythical villain in *The Usual Suspects*

175

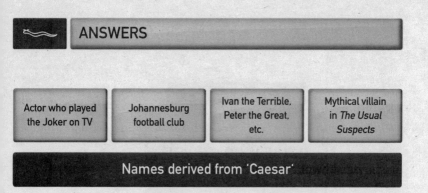

| Actor who played the Joker on TV | Johannesburg football club | Ivan the Terrible, Peter the Great, etc. | Mythical villain in *The Usual Suspects* |

Names derived from 'Caesar'

- The Joker was played by CESAR Romero.
- Johannesburg football club: KAIZER Chiefs, named after founder Kaizer Motaung. The Leeds band Kaiser Chiefs take their name from the team (with one letter changed) inspired by Leeds Utd's Lucas Radebe who had previously played for Kaizer Chiefs.
- CZARS of Russia: 'Caesar' came to have the general sense 'emperor' in a Germanic language, which became the Slavonic word 'czar', which the Russians borrowed.
- Villain in *The Usual Suspects*: KEYSER Söze.

The Psmiths couldn't piece this together, but their opponents the Cosmopolitans picked up a bonus point.

5 points

3 points

2 points

1 point

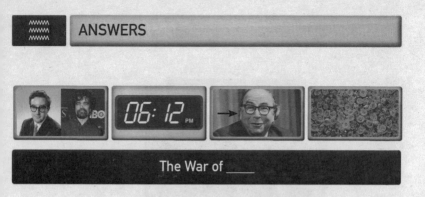

The War of _____

- Peter Sellers and Peter Dinklage: the War of the Two Peters (*Guerra de los dos Pedros*), the Peters being Peter of Castile vs Peter IV of Aragon.
- 6.12pm: the War of 1812, inconclusive war between USA and Britain, 1812–15.
- Roy Jenkins' ear: The War of Jenkins' Ear, merged into the War of the Spanish Succession. According to Robert Jenkins, master of the ship *Rebecca*, he had his ear cut off by Spanish coastguards in 1731, leading to the war.
- Some roses: the War(s) of the Roses, York vs Lancaster. The wars are named after the rose emblems of the two houses.

In the 2016 Comic Relief special, the BBC (Hugh Dennis, Julian Lloyd Webber, Lynne Truss) picked up 2 points on this.

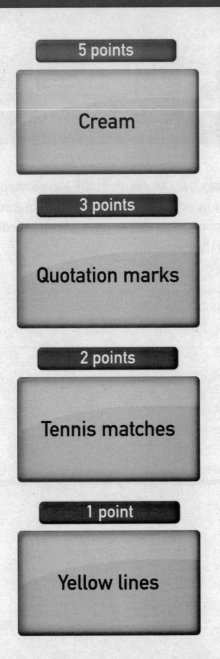

5 points

Cream

3 points

Quotation marks

2 points

Tennis matches

1 point

Yellow lines

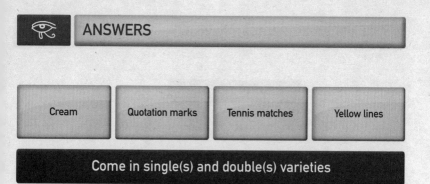

ANSWERS

| Cream | Quotation marks | Tennis matches | Yellow lines |

Come in single(s) and double(s) varieties

All the way back in series 3, the Neuroscientists and their opponents the Rugby Boys (featuring Mark Labbett, now of *The Chase*) both failed to score on this.

5 points

3 points

2 points

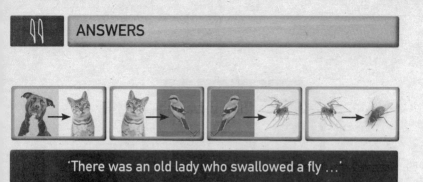

'There was an old lady who swallowed a fly ...'

They are the items in 'There was an old lady who swallowed a fly' and what she swallowed to catch the previous animal or insect

- 'There was an old lady who swallowed a dog / What a hog! To swallow a dog! / She swallowed the dog to catch the cat / She swallowed the cat to catch the bird / She swallowed the bird to catch the spider that wriggled and jiggled and tickled inside her / She swallowed the spider to catch the fly / But I don't know why she swallowed the fly / Perhaps she'll die'.
- Later items are a goat, a cow and a horse. She's dead, of course.
- The lyrics were written by Rose Bonne and the tune by Canadian folksinger Alan Mills.

The Athenians scored 3 points on this in their match against the Roadtrippers.

5 points

5th: AltaVista

3 points

4th: YouTube

2 points

3rd: McDonald's

?

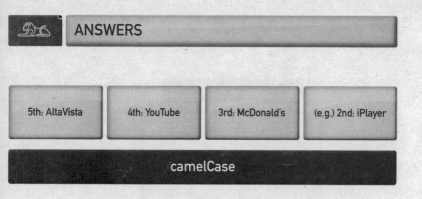

5th: AltaVista | 4th: YouTube | 3rd: McDonald's | (e.g.) 2nd: iPlayer

camelCase

ACCEPT: eBay, iTunes, anything of the form xXxx with a capital second letter

- These brand names have a capital letter in fifth, fourth, third and second place.
- It is known as 'camelCase' because of the humps.
- It is also known as bicapitalisation, medial cap, medial capitals, Pascal case, embedded caps, InterCaps and midcaps.

In the series 10 final, neither the Chessmen nor the Orienteers scored a point on this.

5 points

31,102 verses

3 points

1,189 chapters

2 points

66 books

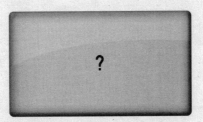

?

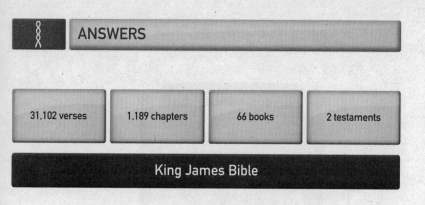

| 31,102 verses | 1,189 chapters | 66 books | 2 testaments |

King James Bible

- Over 780,000 words = 31,102 verses = 1,189 chapters = 66 books = 2 testaments.

The Railwaymen picked up 2 points for this in their series 11 match against the Collectors.

5 points

Formerly UKTV History

3 points

Britain's first full-colour newspaper

2 points

Song from *Annie*

?

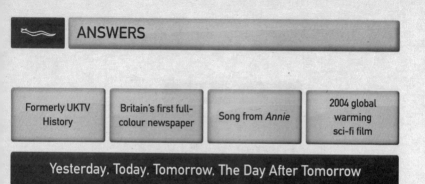

| Formerly UKTV History | Britain's first full-colour newspaper | Song from *Annie* | 2004 global warming sci-fi film |

Yesterday, Today, Tomorrow, The Day After Tomorrow

- Yesterday: TV channel previously called UKTV History. Renamed in 2009.
- *Today*: published between 1986 and 1995.
- 'Tomorrow': '... you're always a day away'.
- *The Day After Tomorrow*: 2004 science-fiction disaster film about the ushering in of a new global ice age. Starred Dennis Quaid and Jake Gyllenhaal.

In the 2013 Children in Need special, the Scrabblers (John Finnemore, Alice Arnold, Konnie Huq) got 3 points on this against the Balding Team (Simon Jenkins, Clare Balding, Clive Anderson).

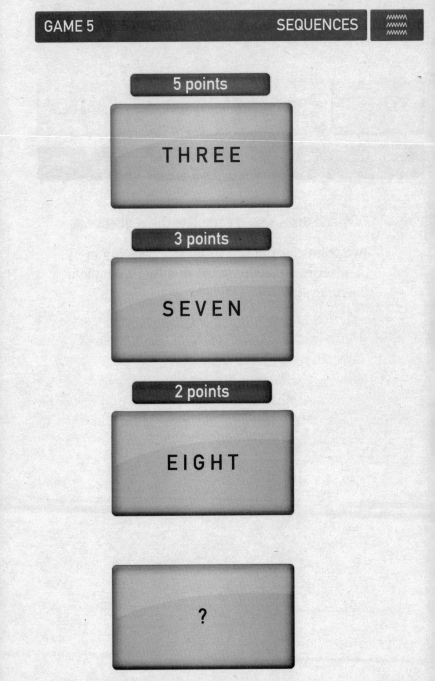

5 points

THREE

3 points

SEVEN

2 points

EIGHT

?

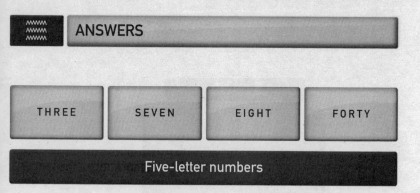

| THREE | SEVEN | EIGHT | FORTY |

Five-letter numbers

Fifty and Sixty would complete the sequence.

Two points for the Editors on this question in their series 5 match against eventual champions, the Analysts.

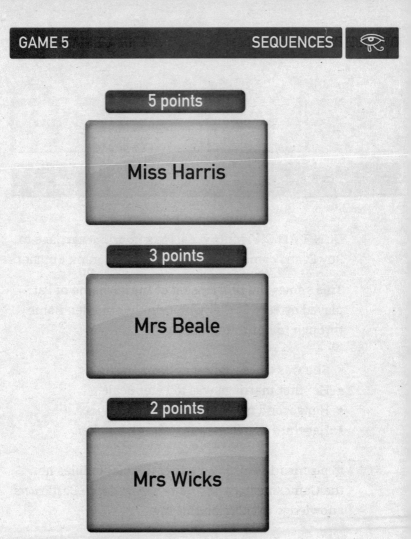

5 points

Miss Harris

3 points

Mrs Beale

2 points

Mrs Wicks

?

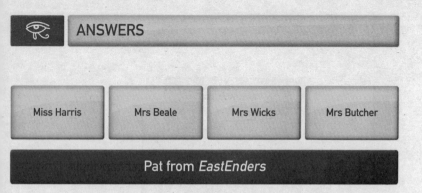

| Miss Harris | Mrs Beale | Mrs Wicks | Mrs Butcher |

Pat from *EastEnders*

DON'T ALLOW: Mrs Evans. Pat's (fourth) marriage to Roy Evans came after her marriage to Frank Butcher

This shows the progression of the surname of Pat, played by Pam St Clement, from her maiden name through to her third marriage

- She was the daughter of Lydia Harris.
- Her first marriage was to Peter Beale.
- Her second marriage was to Brian Wicks.
- Her third marriage was to Frank Butcher.

In a series 10 episode, neither the Bibliophiles nor the Gamesmasters had quite the in-depth *EastEnders* knowledge to score on this one.

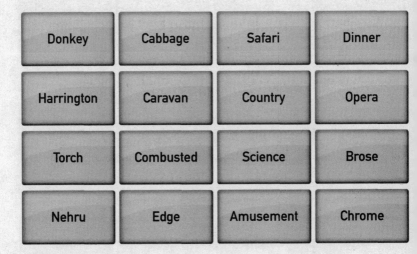

Donkey	Cabbage	Safari	Dinner
Harrington	Caravan	Country	Opera
Torch	Combusted	Science	Brose
Nehru	Edge	Amusement	Chrome

CLUE WORDS

In the same group: Chrome and Torch

In the same group: Combusted and Brose

Not in the same group: Opera and Dinner

Not in the same group: Amusement and Science

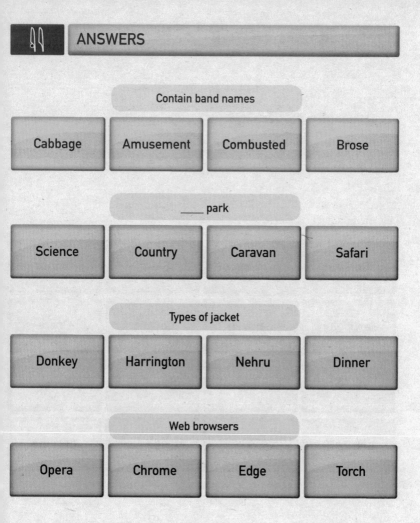

Contain band names

| Cabbage | Amusement | Combusted | Brose |

_____ park

| Science | Country | Caravan | Safari |

Types of jacket

| Donkey | Harrington | Nehru | Dinner |

Web browsers

| Opera | Chrome | Edge | Torch |

The Networkers scored 4 points on this wall.

Wraith	Boulevard	Corniche	Neuron
Shade	Superstar	Trouble	Phantom
Aspects	Spook	Silver Ghost	Spectre
Revenant	Franco	Camargue	Starlight

CLUE WORDS

In the same group: Corniche and Silver Ghost

In the same group: Neuron and Franco

Not in the same group: Aspects and Boulevard

Not in the same group: Spook and Phantom

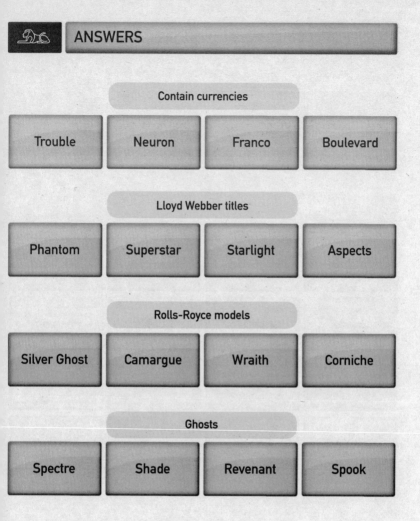

Contain currencies

| Trouble | Neuron | Franco | Boulevard |

Lloyd Webber titles

| Phantom | Superstar | Starlight | Aspects |

Rolls-Royce models

| Silver Ghost | Camargue | Wraith | Corniche |

Ghosts

| Spectre | Shade | Revenant | Spook |

The Cousins picked up 7 on this wall

Basic vocabulary in English and French

HL LN DBNJ R

DGN DC HN

Y SN D

NN D NN

Basic vocabulary in English and French

HL LN DBNJ R

HELLO AND BONJOUR

DGN DC HN

DOG AND CHIEN

Y SN D

YES AND OUI

NN D NN

NO AND NON

Basic vocabulary in English and Italian

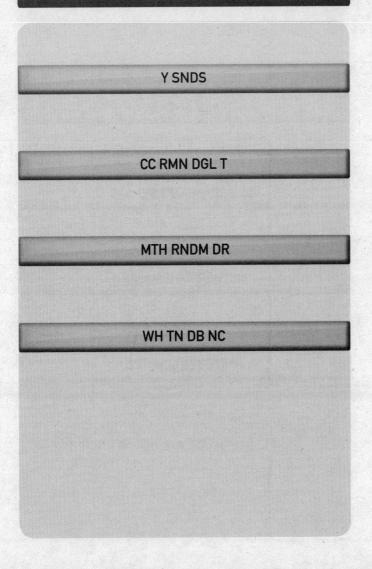

Y SNDS

CC RMN DGL T

MTH RNDM DR

WH TN DB NC

Basic vocabulary in English and Italian

Y SNDS

YES AND SI

CC RMN DGL T

ICE CREAM AND GELATO

MTH RNDM DR

MOTHER AND MADRE

WH TN DB NC

WHITE AND BIANCO

Basic vocabulary in English and German

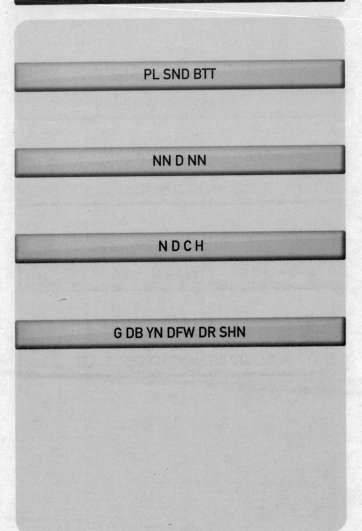

PL SND BTT

NN D NN

N D C H

G DB YN DFW DR SHN

Basic vocabulary in English and German

PL SND BTT

PLEASE AND BITTE

NN D NN

NO AND NEIN

N D C H

I AND ICH

G DB YN DFW DR SHN

GOODBYE AND AUF WIEDERSEHEN

Basic vocabulary in English and Spanish

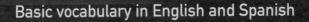

Y SN DS

DNTS PKS PNS HND NHBL SPÑL

HTN DSM BRR

PL SN DPRF VR

Basic vocabulary in English and Spanish

Y SN DS

YES AND SÍ

DNTS PKS PNS HND NHBL SPÑL

I DON'T SPEAK SPANISH AND NO HABLO ESPAÑOL

HTN DSM BRR

HAT AND SOMBRERO

PL SN DPRF VR

PLEASE AND POR FAVOR

Charlie Higson

5 points	3 points	2 points	1 point
The Glass Key	The Scarlett Stiletto	The Macavity	The Gold Dagger

'I can't believe we got this question about crime-writing awards wrong. I've been a judge on the Steel Dagger – a sister award to the Gold Dagger – and my team-mate Daisy Goodwin should have recognised the Macavity, as her brother, Jason, has won the bloody thing! But once your brain starts running along a fixed track it's hard to divert it. All I could think about was Dashiell Hammett, who wrote *The Glass Key*.'

Awards for writing crime fiction

GAME 6

DIFFICULTY LEVEL: 2

5 points

Icelandic: Bra Bra

3 points

Danish: Rap Rap

2 points

French: Coin Coin

1 point

Greek:
Κουάκ Κουάκ

| Icelandic: Bra Bra | Danish: Rap Rap | French: Coin Coin | Greek: Κουάκ Κουάκ |

Non-English speaking ducks

This is what people who speak other languages say for 'quack quack'

The French also sometimes say 'couac couac', but 'coin coin' is the norm.

A bonus point on this baffling question for the Highgates against the Shutterbugs.

5 points

Auto Trader
(2013)

3 points

The Dandy
(2012)

2 points

*Encyclopædia
Britannica*
(2010)

1 point

The Independent
(2016)

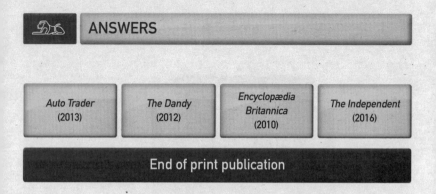

Auto Trader (2013)	*The Dandy* (2012)	*Encyclopædia Britannica* (2010)	*The Independent* (2016)

End of print publication

- *Auto Trader*: print classified ads were no longer a sustainable funding model.
- The *Dandy*: Paul McCartney fulfilled a 'lifelong ambition' by appearing in the final print edition.
- *Encyclopædia Britannica*: after 244 years and dozens of editions, the 32 volumes of the 2010 edition were the last in print.
- The last print edition of the *Independent* was published on Saturday, 26 March 2016.

The Shutterbugs and the Highgates again – this time it was 2 points for the Shutterbugs (though we've slightly adjusted the question for the book).

5 points

Apt

3 points

Apposite

2 points

Awl

1 point

Anion

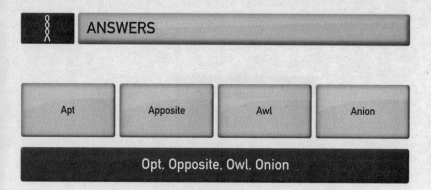

| Apt | Apposite | Awl | Anion |

Opt, Opposite, Owl, Onion

They can all form another word with the initial A changed to an O. Simple as that ...

Two points for the Chessmen against the Linguists.

5 points

Ship of Theseus

3 points

The Sugababes

2 points

George Washington's axe

1 point

Trigger's broom

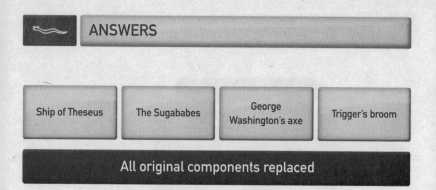

| Ship of Theseus | The Sugababes | George Washington's axe | Trigger's broom |

All original components replaced

- As originally recorded by Plutarch, the Ship of Theseus embodies the paradox of whether something which has had all parts replaced is the same thing.
- Founding members of the Sugababes Siobhán Donaghy, Mutya Buena and Keisha Buchanan left to be replaced in turn by Heidi Range, Amelle Berrabah and Jade Ewen. The three original Sugababes later formed their own band, called MKS.
- Apocryphal story: an axe of George Washington's which had both head and handle replaced but was still regarded as a valuable artefact that once belonged to George Washington.
- In *Only Fools and Horses*, Trigger says his broom had had 17 new heads and 14 new handles.

Three valuable points on this question for the Policy Wonks against the Beekeepers. A very nice example of four 'apparently random' clues ...

5 points

Academic bookseller, est. 1751

3 points

Tadcaster brewer

2 points

Man saved by Pocahontas

1 point

Labour party leader, 1992–4

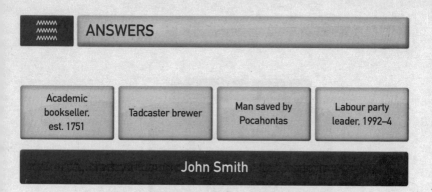

Academic bookseller, est. 1751 | Tadcaster brewer | Man saved by Pocahontas | Labour party leader, 1992–4

John Smith

- John Smith started as a bookseller in Glasgow in 1751.
- John Smith set up his eponymous brewery in 1847.
- Lincolnshire-born explorer and American colonist John Smith (1580–1631) claimed that Pocahontas twice saved his life when he was at the mercy of her tribe.
- John Smith, who took over from Neil Kinnock after Labour's 1992 defeat, died of a heart attack two years later.

No points for either the Accountants or the Cinephiles in this series 6 question.

5 points

Miedinger &
Hoffmann

3 points

Hoefler &
Frere-Jones

2 points

John Baskerville

1 point

Eric Gill

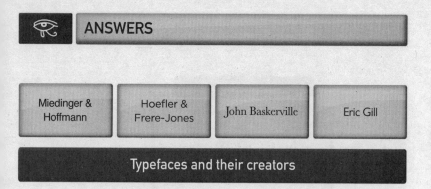

| Miedinger & Hoffmann | Hoefler & Frere-Jones | John Baskerville | Eric Gill |

Typefaces and their creators

- Max Miedinger and Eduard Hoffmann, in Helvetica.
- Jonathan Hoefler and Tobias Frere-Jones, in Gotham – this was used in Obama's 'Hope' campaign.
- John Baskerville, in New Baskerville.
- Eric Gill, in Gill Sans.

Two points for the Nightwatchmen (a rather glittery team in our regular series, featuring football journalist Jonathan Wilson, *Test Match Special*'s Daniel Norcross, and author Robert Winder).

5 points

4: Titov

3 points

3: Grissom

2 points

2: Shepard

?

| 4: Titov | 3: Grissom | 2: Shepard | 1: Gagarin |

First four people in space

- Fourth was Gherman Titov – 6 August 1961.
- Third was Virgil 'Gus' Grissom – 21 July 1961. (William Petersen's character in CSI, Gil Grissom, is named after him).
- Second was Alan Shepard – 5 May 1961 (he played golf on the moon a decade later).
- First was Yuri Gagarin – 12 April 1961.

In series 6, this question went to the Educators. They missed out, however, and their opponents the Wordsmiths picked up a bonus point.

5 points

Franklin D. Roosevelt

3 points

Harry S. Wallace

2 points

Dwight D. Doud

?

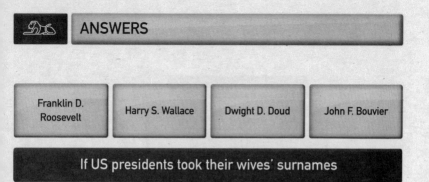

| Franklin D. Roosevelt | Harry S. Wallace | Dwight D. Doud | John F. Bouvier |

If US presidents took their wives' surnames

- Franklin D. Roosevelt (married to Eleanor Roosevelt, his fifth cousin, once removed).
- Harry S. Truman (married to Bess Wallace).
- Dwight D. Eisenhower (married to Mamie Doud).
- John F. Kennedy (married to Jacqueline Bouvier).

This question proved to be beyond the Korfballers and their opponents the Fire-Eaters.

5 points

2:43:38

3 points

3:49:05

2 points

4:54:33

?

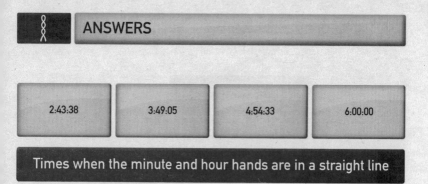

| 2:43:38 | 3:49:05 | 4:54:33 | 6:00:00 |

Times when the minute and hour hands are in a straight line

ACCEPT: 6 o'clock, 6am, 6pm

The Booksellers did not get to the answer in time, and their opponents the Bowlers scored a bonus point.

A deceptively simple question. It looks like it could be something to do with best times for running a marathon …

5 points

3 points

2 points

?

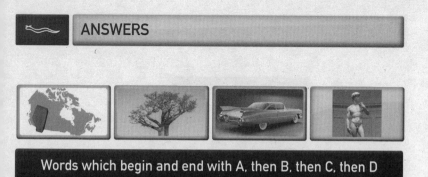

Words which begin and end with A, then B, then C, then D

ACCEPT: anything that represents a word that starts and ends with D

- Alberta, Canadian province.
- Baobab tree.
- Cadillac car.
- David, as depicted by Michelangelo.

A bonus point for the Yorkers against the Operational Researchers.

5 points

Cover 174 feet

3 points

Roll over the boundary

2 points

Hit a helmet on the field

?

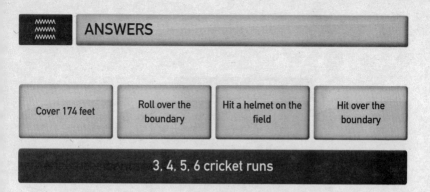

| Cover 174 feet | Roll over the boundary | Hit a helmet on the field | Hit over the boundary |

3, 4, 5, 6 cricket runs

ACCEPT: any situation that is worth 6 runs in cricket (e.g. 'Cover 348 feet', 'Run two, being sure to cross twice (ideally before the fielder throws the ball), and then have the ball ricochet unintentionally off the bat of the diving batsman, and go over the boundary.').

- The distance between the two popping creases, three times – three runs.
- Four runs.
- If the ball hits a helmet on the field (e.g. stored behind the wicketkeeper when nobody is wearing it), five runs are awarded to the batting team.
- Six runs.

In series 4, the Urban Walkers failed to score on this, and their opponents the Wrights picked up a bonus point.

5 points

Monday: met

3 points

Tuesday: went for drink

2 points

Wednesday: made love

?

| Monday: met | Tuesday: went for drink | Wednesday: made love | Thursday: made love |

Craig David's week

ACCEPT: if the answer is given before Wednesday then, generously, 'Sunday: chilled' may be accepted (as the couple were making love on Wednesday, Thursday, Friday and Saturday, so 'chilled on Sunday' is the next different activity mentioned; Clue 3 could conceivably have been 'Wednesday–Saturday: made love')

These are the activities, on successive days, of the narrator and the girl he meets in the Craig David song '7 Days'

Lyrics are …

'I met this girl on Monday / took her for a drink on Tuesday / we were making love by Wednesday … / … and on Thursday and Friday and Saturday; we chilled on Sunday.'

The Polyglots showed excellent Craig David knowledge by scoring 2 points on this against the Yorkers. The crowd said 'Bo Selecta'.

0	16⅔	10	1066
32	33⅓	1830	300
78	1087	2012	273.15
491.67	45	1689	Infinity

CLUE WORDS

In the same group: 16⅔ and 78

In the same group: 0 and 491.67

Not in the same group: 2012 and 1830

Not in the same group: 32 and 45

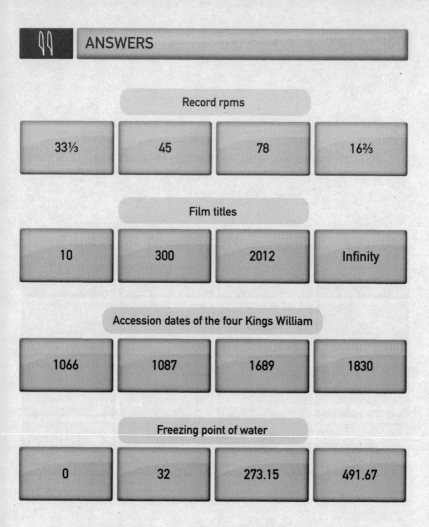

Record rpms

| 33⅓ | 45 | 78 | 16⅔ |

Film titles

| 10 | 300 | 2012 | Infinity |

Accession dates of the four Kings William

| 1066 | 1087 | 1689 | 1830 |

Freezing point of water

| 0 | 32 | 273.15 | 491.67 |

This was part of a pair of horrible-looking walls in the final of series 12 (see below for the other). The Verbivores, who won the series, scored 10 on this one.

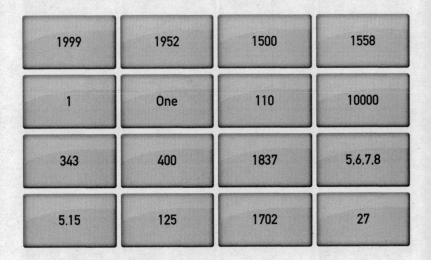

1999	1952	1500	1558
1	One	110	10000
343	400	1837	5,6,7,8
5.15	125	1702	27

CLUE WORDS

In the same group: 27 and 343

In the same group: One and 5, 6, 7, 8

Not in the same group: 1999 and 1952

Not in the same group: 1 and 110

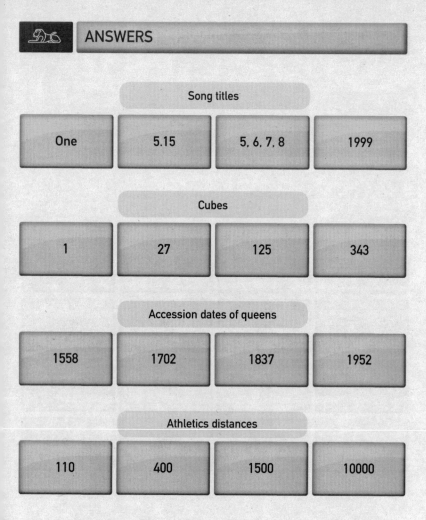

Song titles

| One | 5.15 | 5, 6, 7, 8 | 1999 |

Cubes

| 1 | 27 | 125 | 343 |

Accession dates of queens

| 1558 | 1702 | 1837 | 1952 |

Athletics distances

| 110 | 400 | 1500 | 10000 |

This was the other horrible-looking wall in the final of series 12 (see above for the other). The Cosmopolitans scored 10 on this one.

Cartoon dogs and their owners

S NPYN DCH RLB RWN

SC BYD NDS HG GY

D GB RTN DDL BRT

SN TSL TTL HL PRND THS MPSNS

Cartoon dogs and their owners

S NPYN DCH RLB RWN

SNOOPY AND CHARLIE BROWN

SC BYD NDS HG GY

SCOOBY-DOO AND SHAGGY

D GB RTN DDL BRT

DOGBERT AND DILBERT

SN TSL TTL HL PRND THS MPSNS

SANTA'S LITTLE HELPER AND THE SIMPSONS

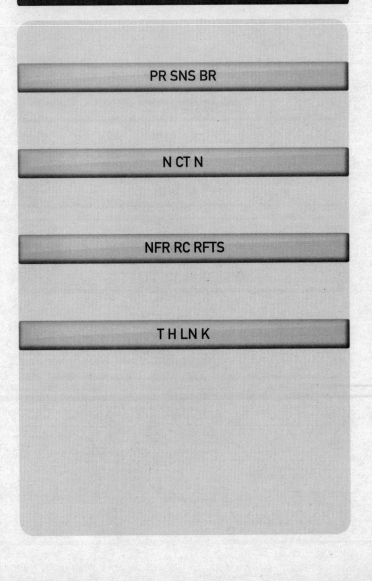

The word 'missing' is missing

PR SNS BR

N CT N

NFR RC RFTS

T H LN K

The word 'missing' is missing

PR SNS BR

PERSONS BUREAU

N CT N

IN ACTION

NFR RC RFTS

ONE OF OUR AIRCRAFT IS

T H LN K

THE LINK

Overlapping country names

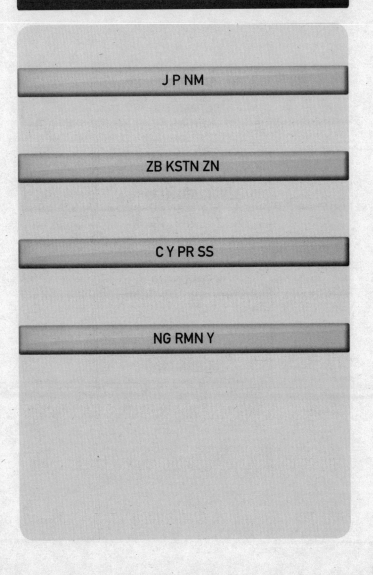

J P NM

ZB KSTN ZN

C Y PR SS

NG RMN Y

Overlapping country names

J P NM

JAPANAMA

ZB KSTN ZN

UZBEKISTANZANIA

C Y PR SS

CYPRUSSIA

NG RMN Y

NIGERMANY

Famous last lines from films

TH RSNP LCL KHM

THH RRR THH RRR

T MR RWS NTH RDY

FRG TTJ KTS CHN TWN

Famous last lines from films

TH RSNP LCL KHM

THERE'S NO PLACE LIKE HOME

THH RRR THH RRR

THE HORROR ... THE HORROR

T MR RWS NTH RDY

TOMORROW IS ANOTHER DAY

FRG TTJ KTS CHN TWN

FORGET IT JAKE, IT'S CHINATOWN

- *The Wizard of Oz*
- *Apocalypse Now*
- *Gone with the Wind*
- *Chinatown*

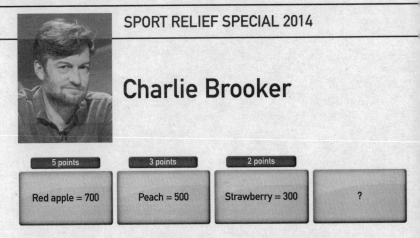

Charlie Brooker

5 points	3 points	2 points	
Red apple = 700	Peach = 500	Strawberry = 300	?

'I remember being fairly cowed by the knowledge that my team-mates had displayed in advance, and thinking, "I'm going to look like a real thicko." But then quite early on, a question came up about Pac-Man and I thought "Oh good, I'm in my element."'

Cherries = 100. (Fruits in *Pac-Man* by points value)

GAME 7

DIFFICULTY LEVEL: 3

5 points

Country:
South Africa

3 points

UK county:
Northamptonshire

2 points

UK region:
East Anglia

1 point

US state:
West Virginia

| Country: South Africa | UK county: Northamptonshire | UK region: East Anglia | US state: West Virginia |

No directional counterparts

For each of these clues, you cannot replace the compass point with any other to get a related geographical entity

- There is no country called West, North or East Africa.
- There is no UK county called East, Sout(h) or West ____hamptonshire.
- There is no UK region called South, West or North Anglia.
- There is no US state called North, East or South Virginia.

The Yorkers scored a point on this question in their series 11 battle against the Wayfarers.

5 points

Inferno

3 points

Prometheus Bound

2 points

I Am Not Spock

1 point

Paradise Lost

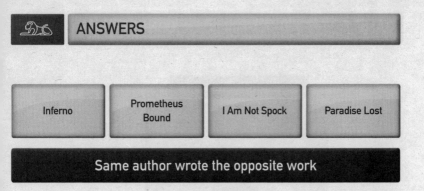

| Inferno | Prometheus Bound | I Am Not Spock | Paradise Lost |

Same author wrote the opposite work

- Dante: *Inferno* and *Paradiso*.
- Aeschylus: *Prometheus Bound* and *Prometheus Unbound*.
- Leonard Nimoy: *I Am Not Spock* and *I Am Spock*.
- John Milton: *Paradise Lost* and *Paradise Regained*.

A point for the Radio Addicts against the Epicureans in the series 4 final.

5 points

3 points

2 points

1 point

Homophones of Roman numerals

ACCEPT: Homphones of two letters

- The lemur called an aye-aye = II = 2.
- Ivy = IV = 4.
- Blunt Wetherton copper Dalziel (played by Warren Clarke) from *Dalziel and Pascoe* = DL = 550.
- (Microsoft) Excel = XL = 40.

2 points for the Surrealists against the Genealogists.

5 points

Two UK no.1 artists: Manic Street Preachers

3 points

Two Elements: Platinum

2 points

Two Greek letters: Upsilon

1 point

Two countries: Somalia

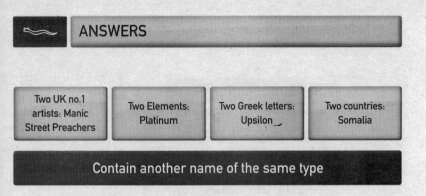

| Two UK no.1 artists: Manic Street Preachers | Two Elements: Platinum | Two Greek letters: Upsilon | Two countries: Somalia |

Contain another name of the same type

- Manic Street PreaCHERs contains Cher (e.g. 'If You Tolerate This Your Children Will Be Next', and 'Believe').
- PlaTINum contains Tin.
- UPSIlon contains Psi.
- SoMALIa contains Mali.

One point for the Wayfarers against the Yorkers.

5 points

Syphilis

3 points

Sweating sickness

2 points

Rickets

1 point

Football
hooliganism

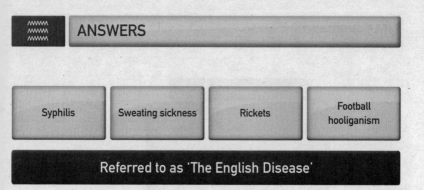

| Syphilis | Sweating sickness | Rickets | Football hooliganism |

Referred to as 'The English Disease'

- Syphilis: a sexually transmitted infection, aka the French/Spanish/German/Polish/Christian Disease.
- Sweating sickness: mysterious and highly virulent disease that struck England in 1485.
- Rickets: softening of bones due to deficiency of vitamin D, calcium or phosphate.
- Football hooliganism: England had a worldwide reputation for trouble at matches in the 1970s and 1980s.

The three actual diseases in the question were labelled because they were endemic at some point in history in England or considered to have originated there or by means of English people.

The Gamesmasters scored a point on this question in their series 10 match against the Orienteers.

5 points

Jason

3 points

My dame

2 points

Brian Whittle

1 point

Cinderella

259

| Jason | My dame | Brian Whittle | Cinderella |

Lost footwear

- In the Greek myth, Jason loses a sandal in a river, fulfilling a prophecy that King Pelias must beware a man with one sandal.
- The dame loses her shoe in the nursery rhyme 'Cock a Doodle Do!' 'Cock a doodle doo! My dame has lost her shoe, My master's lost his fiddling-stick, And doesn't know what to do.'
- Scottish athlete Brian Whittle lost a shoe during his leg of the 1986 European 4 × 400-metre relay final, but carried on in his sock (and his GB team won!).
- In the best known version of the Cinderella fairy tale, by Charles Perrault, the heroine loses her glass slipper running from the ball.

In series 9, the Welsh Learners scored 2 points against the Relatives on this question.

5 points

Extra

3 points

Roadchef

2 points

Welcome Break

?

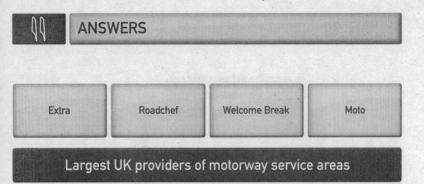

Extra	Roadchef	Welcome Break	Moto

Largest UK providers of motorway service areas

- Extra operates 7 Motorway Service Areas (+ 3 more if you count A1M Baldock, A14 (M11) Cambridge and A1M Peterborough).
- Roadchef operates 21 Motorway Service Areas.
- Welcome Break operates 25 Motorway Service Areas (plus a few A-road ones, and some jointly with Extra).
- Moto has 49 Motorway Service Areas (if you include the ones on opposite sides of the motorway as one each; even if you don't, they still have the most).

2 points for the Spaghetti Westerners against the Mixologists. This is the Series Producer's favourite *Only Connect* question of all time. Make of that what you will …

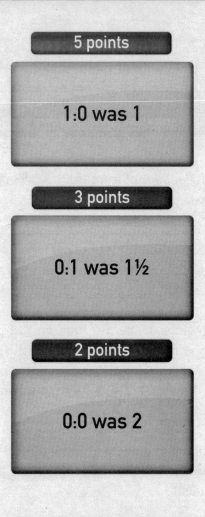

5 points

1:0 was 1

3 points

0:1 was 1½

2 points

0:0 was 2

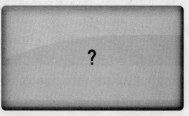

?

| 1:0 was 1 | 0:1 was 1½ | 0:0 was 2 | (e.g.) 1:1 was 3 |

Football pools

ACCEPT: any answer of form X:X = 3, where X is bigger than 0

These were the points, in ascending value, given for match outcomes in the classic (and most famous) scoring system in the 'Treble Chance' football pools game. Nowadays just 1 point is given for an away win.

- A 'home win' (such as 1–0) was worth 1 point.
- An 'away win' (such as 0–1) was worth 1½ points.
- A 'no-score draw' (i.e. 0–0) was worth 2 points.
- A 'score draw' (1–1, 2–2, 3–3, etc.) was worth 3 points.

This question was a no-score draw for the Wayfarers and the Yorkers (which did not result in 2 points being awarded).

5 points

The Saturdays

3 points

Brahma

2 points

Cerberus

?

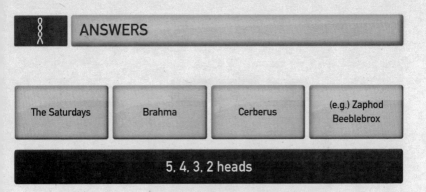

| The Saturdays | Brahma | Cerberus | (e.g.) Zaphod Beeblebrox |

5, 4, 3, 2 heads

ACCEPT: double-headed coin, Orthrus – dog brother of Cerberus, Pushmi-pullyu – from *Doctor Dolittle*, any two-headed group (Wham!, Romeo and Juliet, Tom and Jerry, any twins, etc.)

- The Saturdays are a girl band with five members.
- Each head of the Brahma recites one of the Vedas, a group of ancient Sanskrit texts.
- Cerberus was the three-headed dog who guarded Hades. (Early accounts give him 50 or 100 heads.)
- Zaphod Beeblebrox is a character in *The Hitchhiker's Guide to the Galaxy*.

In series 7, the Corpuscles spotted this on Clue 3, and scored 2 points.

5 points

3 points

2 points

?

Clergy seniority

After centuries of ecclesiastical wrangling, especially between Canterbury and York, this is the order of seniority in the Church of England.

- Fourth is Durham.
- Third is London.
- Second is York.
- First is Canterbury.

No points on this for either the Fire-Eaters or the Verbivores.

5 points

28: 3 in 48

3 points

29: 1 in 48

2 points

30: 16 in 48

?

ANSWERS

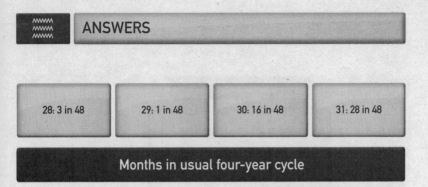

| 28: 3 in 48 | 29: 1 in 48 | 30: 16 in 48 | 31: 28 in 48 |

Months in usual four-year cycle

In a four-year cycle (of 48 months), this is the number of months that have the number of days stated in the clue

- 28: 3/48: there are three 28-day months every four years.
- 29: 1/48: there is one 29-day month every four years.
- 30: 16/48: there are 16 30-day months every four years.
- 31: 28/48: there are 28 31-day months every four years.

Neither the Verbivores nor the Taverners picked up a point on this one. Well done if you got it!

5 points

Ageing

3 points

Aluminium

2 points

Foetus

?

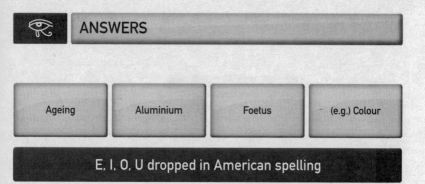

| Ageing | Aluminium | Foetus | (e.g.) Colour |

E, I, O, U dropped in American spelling

ACCEPT: any American word that drops the 'u', including favour/favor, neighbour/neighbor, flavour/flavor, humour/humor, rumour/rumor

- Ageing/aging.
- Aluminium/Aluminum.
- Foetus/Fetus.
- Colour/Color.

The Athenians failed to get this, but their opponents the Road Trippers picked up a bonus point.

The Red Queen	Mrs Miggins	Ascot	Bandana
Ophelia	Fichu	Pukka	Titus Andronicus
Pashmina	Chutney	Bellatrix Lestrange	Cravat
Mrs Bucket	Kerchief	Mrs Lovett	Pyjamas

CLUE WORDS

In the same group: Mrs Lovett and Titus Andronicus

In the same group: The Red Queen and Bellatrix Lestrange

Not in the same group: Pashmina and Cravat

Not in the same group: Bandana and Pukka

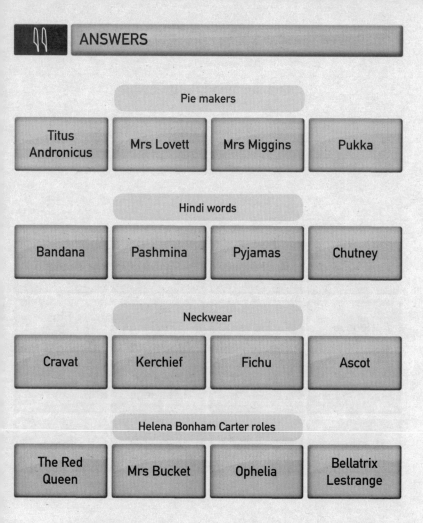

Pie makers

| Titus Andronicus | Mrs Lovett | Mrs Miggins | Pukka |

Hindi words

| Bandana | Pashmina | Pyjamas | Chutney |

Neckwear

| Cravat | Kerchief | Fichu | Ascot |

Helena Bonham Carter roles

| The Red Queen | Mrs Bucket | Ophelia | Bellatrix Lestrange |

The Polyglots scored 6 points on this tricky wall.

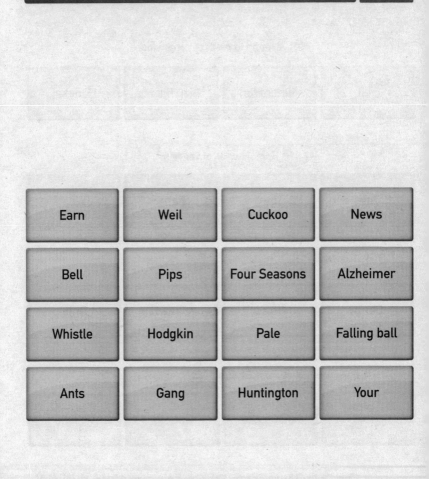

Earn	Weil	Cuckoo	News
Bell	Pips	Four Seasons	Alzheimer
Whistle	Hodgkin	Pale	Falling ball
Ants	Gang	Huntington	Your

CLUE WORDS

In the same group: Gang and Ants
In the same group: Earn and Pale
Not in the same group: Weil and Alzheimer
Not in the same group: Bell and Cuckoo

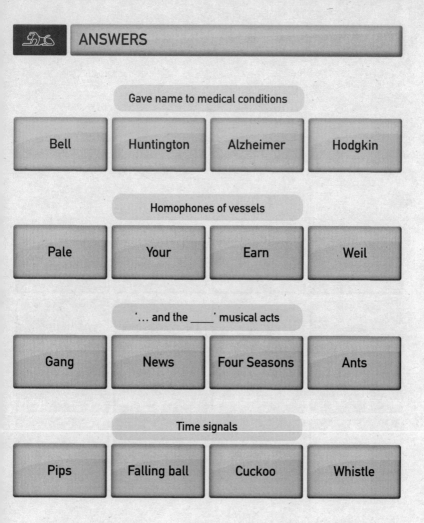

Gave name to medical conditions

| Bell | Huntington | Alzheimer | Hodgkin |

Homophones of vessels

| Pale | Your | Earn | Weil |

'… and the ____' musical acts

| Gang | News | Four Seasons | Ants |

Time signals

| Pips | Falling ball | Cuckoo | Whistle |

The Orienteers scored the maximum 10 on this wall.

Patron saints and what they are patrons of

CRS PNN DCBB LRS

L KN DDC TRS

F RNC SFSSS NDNM LWL FR

VLN TNN DBK PNG

Patron saints and what they are patrons of

CRS PNN DCBB LRS

CRISPIN AND COBBLERS

L KN DDC TRS

LUKE AND DOCTORS

F RNC SFSSS NDNM LWL FR

FRANCIS OF ASSISI AND ANIMAL WELFARE

VLN TNN DBK PNG

VALENTINE AND BEEKEEPING

Five words in alphabetical order

B GBG BGB GBG

PT TNGP TT NG PT TNG PT TN GPTT NG

B LND RBL NDR BLN DRB LND RB LND R

LSTLS TLST LS TLST

Five words in alphabetical order

B GBG BGB GBG

BAG, BEG, BIG, BOG, BUG

PT TNGP TT NG PT TNG PT TN GPTT NG

PATTING, PETTING, PITTING, POTTING, PUTTING

B LND RBL NDR BLN DRB LND RB LND R

BLANDER, BLENDER, BLINDER, BLONDER, BLUNDER

LSTLS TLST LS TLST

LAST, LEST, LIST, LOST, LUST

Can you find any alternative answers?

With the exact same clues, this category could also be 'Six words in alphabetical order'. Good luck with that…

Things a tennis umpire might say

NWB LLSP LS

GM STN DMT CHFD RR

WL LMSW NTH TSSN DHS LCT DTS RV

LD SNDG NT LMN PLY SSS PNDD

Things a tennis umpire might say

NWB LLSP LS

NEW BALLS PLEASE

GM STN DMT CHFD RR

GAME SET AND MATCH FEDERER

WL LMSW NTH TSSN DHS LCT DTS RV

WILLIAMS WON THE TOSS AND
HAS ELECTED TO SERVE

LD SNDG NT LMN PLY SSS PNDD

LADIES AND GENTLEMEN, PLAY IS SUSPENDED

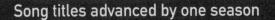

Song titles advanced by one season

HZ YSH DFS PRNG

SM MR TMF RHT LR

TM N TMBLS

W NTRL MNC

Song titles advanced by one season

HZ YSH DFS PRNG

(A) HAZY SHADE OF SPRING

SM MR TMF RHT LR

SUMMERTIME FOR HITLER

TM N TMBLS

AUTUMNTIME BLUES

W NTRL MNC

WINTER ALMANAC

- 'A Hazy Shade of Winter' by The Bangles.
- 'Springtime for Hitler' from the musical *The Producers*.
- 'Summertime Blues' by Eddie Cochran.
- 'Autumn Almanac' by The Kinks.

Val McDermid

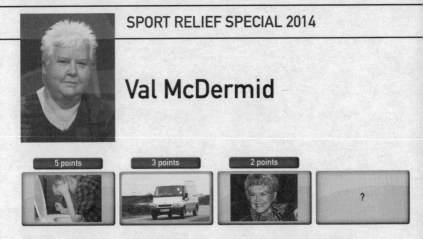

5 points	3 points	2 points	

'My memory is one of schadenfreude. It was the other team's picture question. As soon as I saw the first picture, my brain flashed on the only four-word phrase I knew beginning with "sic" and I just knew the next pic was going to be a Ford Transit. And that's when I eagerly started muttering at Clare Balding, "*Sic Transit Gloria Mundi*!" and she looked at me as if I was barking mad. The other side were completely baffled, and I triumphantly dived in with the answer, chagrined that it hadn't been our question. There is a small coda to this story. My partner Jo was tremendously impressed with this feat until, a couple of years later, we were, as usual, watching QC. First pic, a chocolate bar. "*Picnic at Hanging Rock*!" she shouted. "You might know Latin phrases but I know my chocolate bars!"'

Mundi. (Sic transit gloria mundi).

ACCEPT: a picture of the world, or anything else representing Mundi in some way
• *Sic transit gloria mundi* means 'Thus passes away the glory of the world'.

GAME 8

DIFFICULTY LEVEL: 3

5 points

3 points

2 points

1 point

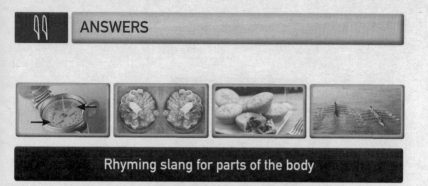

Rhyming slang for parts of the body

- North and south = mouth.
- Plates of meat = feet.
- Mince pies = eyes.
- Boat race = face.

In series 12, the Part-Time Poets made good use of their minces and thought quickly on their plates to score 2 points.

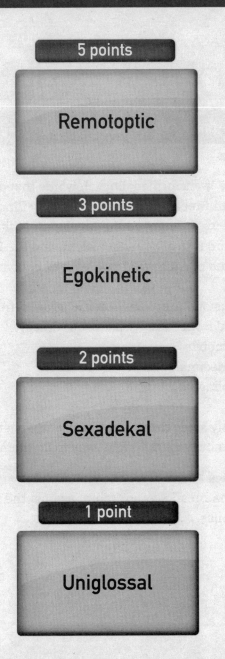

5 points

Remotoptic

3 points

Egokinetic

2 points

Sexadekal

1 point

Uniglossal

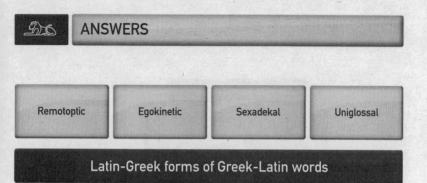

| Remotoptic | Egokinetic | Sexadekal | Uniglossal |

Latin-Greek forms of Greek-Latin words

We have 'transformed' English words that derive half from Greek and half from Latin by flipping them around: we've changed the Greek part at the start of each word into a Latin equivalent, and the Latin part at the end of each word into a Greek equivalent

- Television ('*tele*' from Greek ≈ '*remotus*' from Latin; '*vision*' from Latin ≈ '*optic*' from Greek)
- Automobile
- Hexadecimal
- Monolingual

Obviously since these aren't real words there's no true authority on the 'right' way to do them.

In a series 7 semi-final, the Francophiles (Galliamatores?) scored 1 point against the Cartophiles.

5 points

Bob Hope impersonator

3 points

Physician to inject vitamin B12

2 points

20 white kittens

1 point

M&Ms (no brown ones)

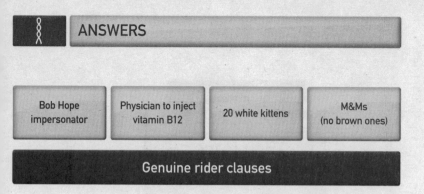

| Bob Hope impersonator | Physician to inject vitamin B12 | 20 white kittens | M&Ms (no brown ones) |

Genuine rider clauses

- Bob Hope impersonator: requested by Iggy Pop.
- Physician to inject vitamin B12: Prince – a famous request in the 1990s.
- 20 white kittens: Mariah Carey – although previously rumoured requests for (e.g.) 'six kittens to stroke' may be an urban myth, she did request kittens to be around her feet (and 100 doves to be released) when turning on the Christmas lights at London's Westfield shopping centre in 2009. The request was refused.
- M&Ms (no brown ones): Van Halen – from 1982. The request was deliberately ridiculous so as to check whether the promoter had followed the small print of the contract properly.

The Antiquarians let this slip, but their opponents the Fantasy Footballers picked up a bonus point.

The grotesquely inflated rider requests of *Only Connect* teams are legendary, ranging all the way from 'a glass of water' to 'a cup of tea, please, if it's not too much trouble'.

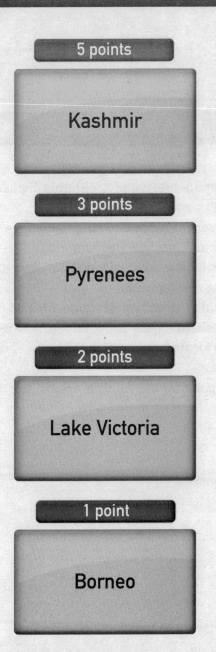

5 points

Kashmir

3 points

Pyrenees

2 points

Lake Victoria

1 point

Borneo

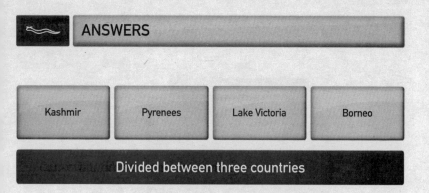

Kashmir	Pyrenees	Lake Victoria	Borneo

Divided between three countries

- The disputed region of Kashmir is divided between India, Pakistan and China.
- The Pyrenees mountain range separates Spain and France, and incorporates Andorra.
- Africa's largest lake is divided between Kenya, Uganda and Tanzania.
- The world's third largest island, divided between Indonesia, Malaysia and Brunei (the latter being wholly located on the island).

A bonus point for the Psmiths against the Wayfarers.

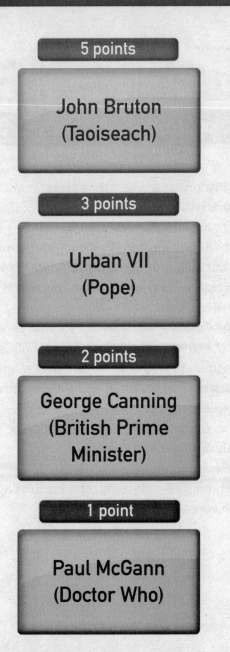

5 points

John Bruton
(Taoiseach)

3 points

Urban VII
(Pope)

2 points

George Canning
(British Prime
Minister)

1 point

Paul McGann
(Doctor Who)

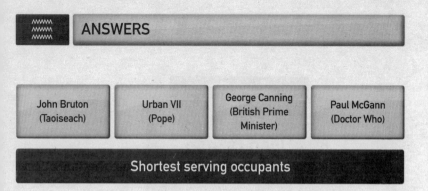

| John Bruton (Taoiseach) | Urban VII (Pope) | George Canning (British Prime Minister) | Paul McGann (Doctor Who) |

Shortest serving occupants

- John Bruton served less than three years as Taoiseach (Irish head of government): December 1994 to June 1997.
- Urban VII was elected Pope on 15 September 1590 but died of malaria 12 days later, before his consecration, and became the shortest serving Pope in history.
- George Canning was Tory PM for four months in 1827 before he died. His advocacy of Catholic emancipation was not popular with many leading politicians, and personal animosities took a toll on his health.
- Paul McGann was the eighth Doctor – he appeared in only one 90-minute episode.

An outstanding 3-pointer for the Psmiths against the Verbivores.

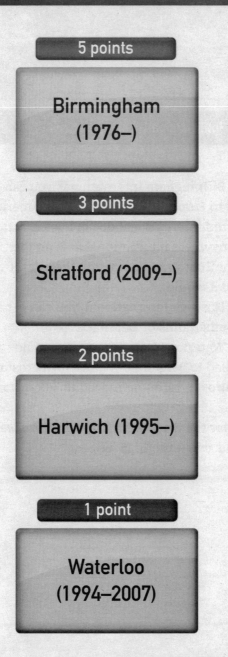

5 points

Birmingham
(1976–)

3 points

Stratford (2009–)

2 points

Harwich (1995–)

1 point

Waterloo
(1994–2007)

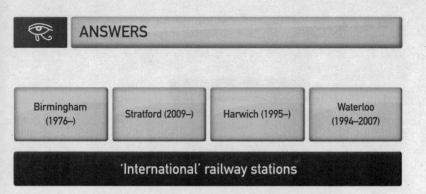

| Birmingham (1976–) | Stratford (2009–) | Harwich (1995–) | Waterloo (1994–2007) |

'International' railway stations

- From Birmingham International, you can get a plane to Europe, Africa, Asia or the Americas.
- Stratford International doesn't actually take you anywhere international. It is on the HS1, but the Eurostar doesn't stop there (as it was hoped it would).
- From Harwich International, you can get a boat to the Netherlands or Denmark.
- From Waterloo International, you could have travelled to Belgium or France (by Eurostar) before the Eurostar terminal moved to St Pancras.

1 point for the Orienteers (knowing their way to get around) against the QI Elves.

5 points

3 points

2 points

?

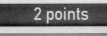

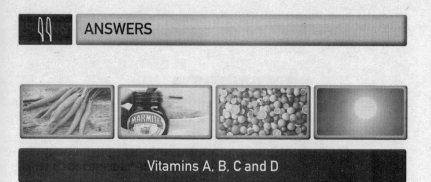

Vitamins A, B, C and D

ACCEPT: liver, fish oils, eggs, vitamin supplements, fortified cereals, fortified milk

- Vitamin A is formed from β-carotene, found in carrots.
- Yeasty spreads such as Marmite contain Vitamin B.
- Humans cannot synthesize vitamin C; the main source is citrus fruits and vegetables.
- Vitamin D is produced in skin exposed to sunlight.

A very impressive 3 points for the Operational Researchers against the Spaghetti Westerners, in the match that holds the record for the longest aggregate number of letters in the teams' names, some way ahead of second place: Cambridge Quiz Society vs Oxford Librarians in series 2, and third place: Edinburgh Scrabblers vs Solent Scrabblers in series 1.

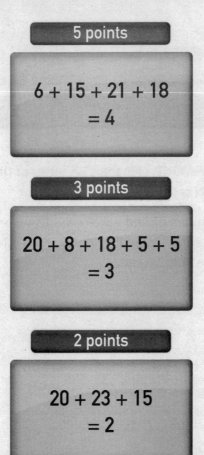

5 points

$$6 + 15 + 21 + 18 = 4$$

3 points

$$20 + 8 + 18 + 5 + 5 = 3$$

2 points

$$20 + 23 + 15 = 2$$

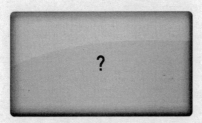

?

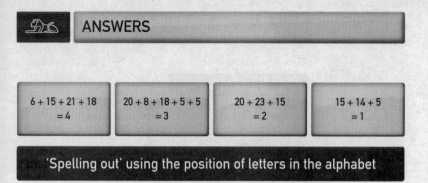

$6 + 15 + 21 + 18$ $= 4$	$20 + 8 + 18 + 5 + 5$ $= 3$	$20 + 23 + 15$ $= 2$	$15 + 14 + 5$ $= 1$

'Spelling out' using the position of letters in the alphabet

For example, ONE: O is the 15th letter of the alphabet, N is the 14th and E is the 5th

The Korfballers picked up $20 + 8 + 18 + 5 + 5$ points on this, in their series $20 + 23 + 5 + 12 + 22 + 5$ match against the Fire-Eaters.

5 points

Magna Carta signing

3 points

Battle of Agincourt

2 points

Vol 2. of *Don Quixote* published

?

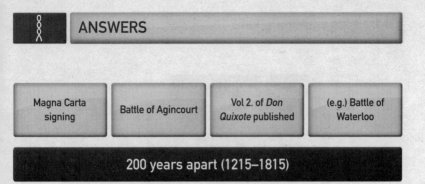

| Magna Carta signing | Battle of Agincourt | Vol 2. of *Don Quixote* published | (e.g.) Battle of Waterloo |

200 years apart (1215–1815)

ACCEPT: 'The Congress of Vienna ends', or anything else that happened in 1815

- Magna Carta signing: 1215.
- Battle of Agincourt: 1415.
- *Don Quixote* by Cervantes: 1615.
- Battle of Waterloo: 1815.

In series 5, the Listeners seized on this for 3 points against the Rowers.

If the sequence were to continue, the most significant event of 2015 for the next clue would be 'The Orienteers win series 10 of *Only Connect*.'

5 points

(e.g.) audio

3 points

(e.g.) lego

2 points

(e.g.) video

?

ANSWERS

| (e.g.) audio | (e.g.) lego | (e.g.) video | (e.g.) amo |

Latin verb conjugations

ACCEPT: any first conjugation Latin verb, e.g. porto, do, lavo

DON'T ACCEPT: any verb from any other conjugation

- *audio* – fourth conjugation, means 'I hear'.
- *lego* – third conjugation, means 'I read'.
- *video* – second conjugation, means 'I see'.
- *amo* – first conjugation, means 'I love'.

3 points on this for the Wayfarers against the Yorkers. When it was on the show, the question was a little easier than this, as each clue was preceded by its conjugation number. We decided to make it harder again for the book.

5 points

Zaireeka

3 points

Sandinista!

2 points

Songs in the Key
of Life

?

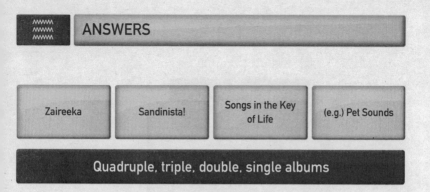

| Zaireeka | Sandinista! | Songs in the Key of Life | (e.g.) Pet Sounds |

Quadruple, triple, double, single albums

ACCEPT: any single album

- *Zaireeka* was a 1997 quadruple album by The Flaming Lips, where each CD was intended to be played simultaneously.
- *Sandinista!* was a 1980 triple album by The Clash.
- *Songs in the Key of Life* was a 1976 double album by Stevie Wonder.
- *Pet Sounds* was a 1966 (single) album by The Beach Boys.

A valuable 2 points for the Athenians in their series 11 match against the Bookworms.

5 points

1.0, 2.0, 3.0

3 points

95, 98, Me

2 points

2000, XP, Vista

?

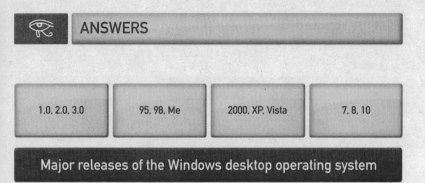

| 1.0, 2.0, 3.0 | 95, 98, Me | 2000, XP, Vista | 7, 8, 10 |

Major releases of the Windows desktop operating system

Microsoft skipped 9 and went to 10; some joke that this is because '7 ate 9'; a more plausible theory is that many existing programs use 'Windows 9' or 'Windows 9X' to refer to the old versions 95 and 98

The Wayfarers unpicked this to score 3 points against the Builders.

Wye	Shag	Twite	Taff
Eye	Sea	Level	Shuttle
Jay	Pea	Pop	Swift
Dee	Deed	Poppy	Usk

CLUE WORDS

In the same group: Dee and Wye

In the same group: Sea and Pea

Not in the same group: Eye and Jay

Not in the same group: Swift and Shuttle

British birds

| Jay | Shag | Swift | Twite |

_____cock

| Poppy | Sea | Pea | Shuttle |

Palindromes

| Eye | Level | Deed | Pop |

Welsh rivers

| Dee | Wye | Usk | Taff |

The Athenians sidestepped most of the tricks lurking in this wall for an impressive 10.

Not	Nit	Livers	Leeds
Shaft	Head	Nock	Snug tent
Deal	Walmer	Nob	Cooling
Fletching	Night	Nave	Hever

CLUE WORDS

In the same group: Nit and Snug tent
In the same group: Nock and Shaft
Not in the same group: Not and Nock
Not in the same group: Hever and Deal

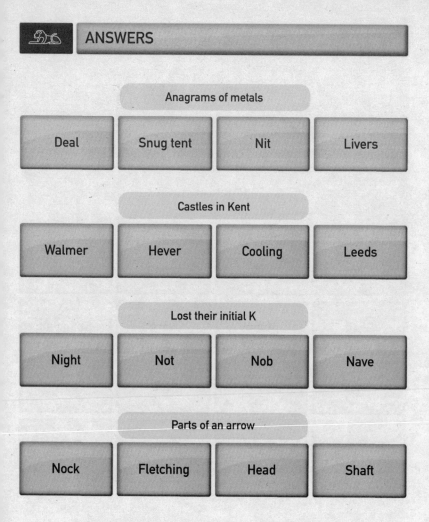

Anagrams of metals

| Deal | Snug tent | Nit | Livers |

Castles in Kent

| Walmer | Hever | Cooling | Leeds |

Lost their initial K

| Night | Not | Nob | Nave |

Parts of an arrow

| Nock | Fletching | Head | Shaft |

The Beekeepers were undone by the anagrams, and ended on 5 points in this tricky series 12 wall.

More or higher is worse

ST RK SNB SB LL

HND CPNG LF

PNT SND RVN GLC NC

CMP LN TS TFCM

More or higher is worse

ST RK SNB SB LL

STRIKES IN BASEBALL

HND CPNG LF

(A) HANDICAP IN GOLF

PNT SND RVN GLC NC

POINTS ON A DRIVING LICENCE

CMP LN TS TFCM

COMPLAINTS TO OFCOM

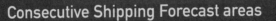

Consecutive Shipping Forecast areas

SLN DLN DY

RC KLL NDM LN

TY NN DD GG R

RS HSN DSH NNN

Consecutive Shipping Forecast areas

SLN DLN DY

SOLE AND LUNDY

RC KLL NDM LN

ROCKALL AND MALIN

TY NN DD GG R

TYNE AND DOGGER

RS HSN DSH NNN

IRISH SEA AND SHANNON

Excuses given by train companies

PN TSF LR

L VSN THLN

VRR NNN GNG NRN GWR KS

W RN GKN DFSN W

Excuses given by train companies

PN TSF LR

POINTS FAILURE

L VSN THLN

LEAVES ON THE LINE

VRR NNN GNG NRN GWR KS

OVERRUNNING ENGINEERING WORKS

W RN GKN DFSN W

WRONG KIND OF SNOW

Film titles decreased by one

T WMN NDB BY

SN WW HTN DTHS XDW RFS

N NHND RDND NN TYN NTHSN DNNH
NDRD NDN NTYN NDL LRB BY

TH SXY RTC H

Film titles decreased by one

T WMN NDB BY

TWO MEN AND A BABY

SN WW HTN DTHS XDW RFS

SNOW WHITE AND THE SIX DWARFS

N NHND RDND NN TYN NTHSN DNNH
NDRD NDN NTYN NDL LRB BY

NINE HUNDRED AND NINETY-NINE THOUSAND NINE
HUNDRED AND NINETY-NINE DOLLAR BABY

W NTRL MNC

THE SIX YEAR ITCH

Clare Balding

BT TRLT TH NNV R

'It was a tie-breaker – captains only. My wife Alice
Arnold was the opposing team captain and we were
both very nervous. We'd played one match already, for
Sport Relief, which I'd won so I genuinely wanted her
to win this one. But as soon as I heard the tie-break
would be missing vowels, I knew I'd got it. I mouthed
"sorry" at her. If it was a numbers question, Alice
would have won. She still minds. It still brings her
out in a cold sweat. It is the hardest I've ever had to
concentrate on a show ever.'

BETTER LATE THAN NEVER

GAME 9

DIFFICULTY LEVEL: 3

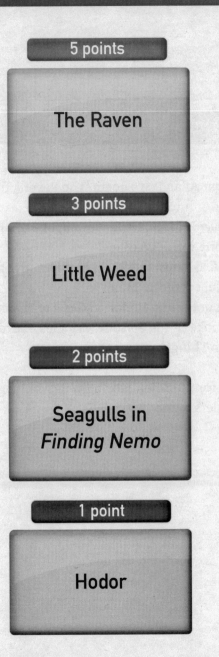

5 points

The Raven

3 points

Little Weed

2 points

Seagulls in *Finding Nemo*

1 point

Hodor

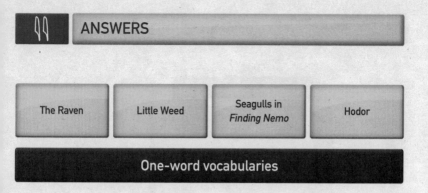

| The Raven | Little Weed | Seagulls in *Finding Nemo* | Hodor |

One-word vocabularies

- In Edgar Allan Poe's poem 'The Raven', the bird only ever intones 'Nevermore'.
- In *Flower Pot Men*, Little Weed spoke to Bill and Ben with one word 'Weeeeed'.
- In *Finding Nemo*, the 2003 Pixar film, the greedy birds just screech 'Mine!'
- Hodor only says 'Hodor' in *Game of Thrones*. He first spoke in the episode 'Cripples, Bastards and Broken Things'.

2 points for the Scientists in their match against the Builders.

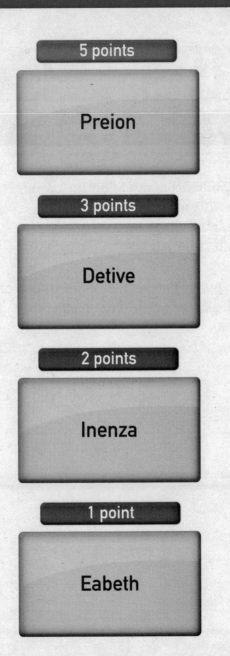

5 points

Preion

3 points

Detive

2 points

Inenza

1 point

Eabeth

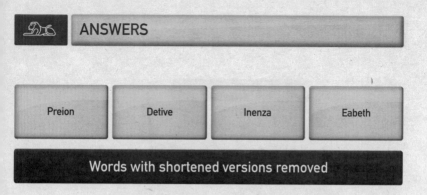

| Preion | Detive | Inenza | Eabeth |

Words with shortened versions removed

- PRESCRIPTION minus SCRIPT.
- DETECTIVE minus TEC.
- INFLUENZA minus FLU.
- ELIZABETH minus LIZ.

2 crucial points for eventual series champions the Verbivores in their semi-final against the Surrealists.

5 points

Claudius, Seneca's *Apocolocyntosis*

3 points

Tomato, 1893 US Supreme Court declaration

2 points

Graham Taylor, *Sun* front page on 24 November 1993

1 point

Carriage at midnight, *Cinderella*

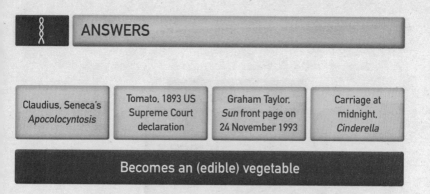

| Claudius, Seneca's *Apocolocyntosis* | Tomato, 1893 US Supreme Court declaration | Graham Taylor, *Sun* front page on 24 November 1993 | Carriage at midnight, *Cinderella* |

Becomes an (edible) vegetable

- Seneca's *Apocolocyntosis* is a vicious satire in which the Emperor Claudius is turned into a pumpkin on his death (*Apocolocyntosis* means Pumpkinification).
- The US Supreme Court declared that, for customs purposes, the tomato was a vegetable, not a fruit.
- *The Sun* headline 'That's Your Allotment' was accompanied by an image of Taylor as a turnip after he resigned as England manager.
- Cinderella's carriage turns back into a pumpkin at midnight.

In series 12, the Wrestlers didn't spot this, but their opponents the Genealogists picked up the bonus.

This is a favourite question of one of the question editors, who was pleased to have a connection between 1990s football and first-century satire.

5 points

Bird

3 points

Little Dyer

2 points

Angelic Brother

1 point

Little Barrel

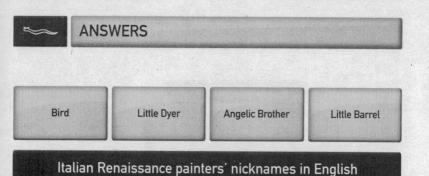

| Bird | Little Dyer | Angelic Brother | Little Barrel |

Italian Renaissance painters' nicknames in English

- 'Uccello' means 'Bird'. Paolo Uccello was born Paolo di Dono.
- 'Tintoretto' means 'Little Dyer'. Tintoretto's real name was Jacopo Comin (aka Jacopo Robusti).
- 'Fra Angelico' means 'Angelic Brother'. He was born Guido di Pietro.
- 'Botticelli' means 'Little Barrel'. Sandro Botticelli was born Alessandro di Mariano di Vanni Filipepi.

In a series 11 semi-final, neither eventual champions the String Section nor their opponents the Cluesmiths worked this out.

5 points

3 points

2 points

1 point

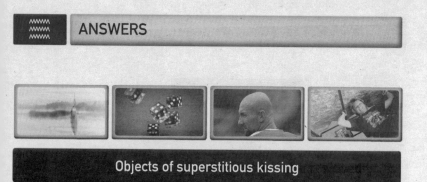

Objects of superstitious kissing

- Superstitious fishermen might kiss a fish for good luck, or as a mark of respect for the fish.
- Many people will kiss the dice before rolling them, hoping for good luck.
- Fabien Barthez was the French goalkeeper whose bald head was kissed by defenders such as Laurent Blanc before matches.
- Legend has it that kissing the Blarney Stone gives the kisser the gift of the gab..

The Fantasy Footballers clocked this after seeing the Fabien Barthez clue to pick up 2 points in a very high-scoring defeat (24–27) against the Antiquarians in series 5.

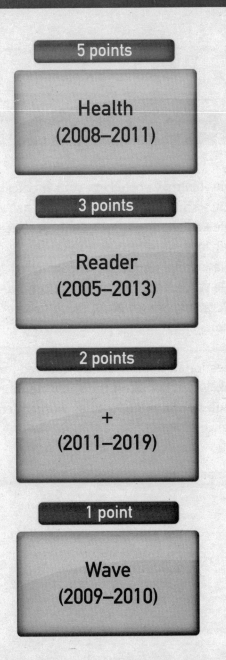

5 points

Health
(2008–2011)

3 points

Reader
(2005–2013)

2 points

+
(2011–2019)

1 point

Wave
(2009–2010)

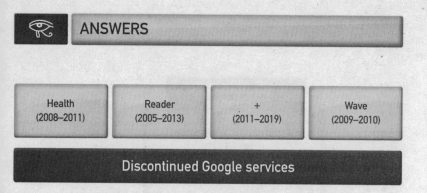

| Health (2008–2011) | Reader (2005–2013) | + (2011–2019) | Wave (2009–2010) |

Discontinued Google services

- Google Health: Google kept your medical records for you – shut down 2011.
- Google Reader: aggregated feeds of content – closed 2013.
- Google+: social network – discontinued 2019.
- Google Wave: Twitter/email/chat combo – development ceased 2010, though some 'Waves' lived on.

This question has been slightly updated for the book. When it was on the show, neither the Nordiphiles nor the Bibliophiles worked it out.

5 points

3 points

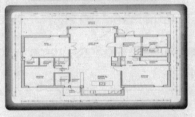

2 points

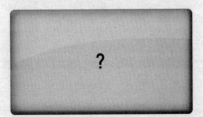

?

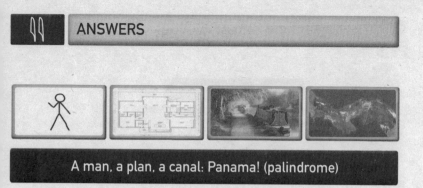

A man, a plan, a canal: Panama! (palindrome)

The answer shown is a satellite image of Panama.

The palindrome was devised by the British recreational mathematician Leigh Mercer.

A complete blank for the Scunthorpe Scholars and the Beekeepers.

5 points

201520

3 points

162017

2 points

201820

?

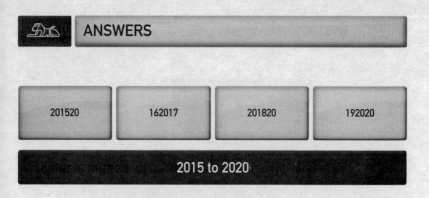

ANSWERS

| 201520 | 162017 | 201820 | 192020 |

2015 to 2020

- 2015 and 20 …
- … 16 and 2017
- 2018 and 20 …
- … 19 and 2020

The Beekeepers did not spot this, but their opponents the Korfballers picked up a bonus point.

One of those fiendishly simple questions that are much harder to spot than they ought to be.

5 points

Lord Redesdale

3 points

Mr Bennet

2 points

Tsar Nicholas II

?

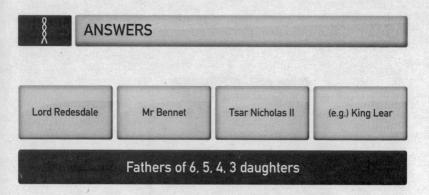

| Lord Redesdale | Mr Bennet | Tsar Nicholas II | (e.g.) King Lear |

Fathers of 6, 5, 4, 3 daughters

ACCEPT: anyone with three daughters

- Lord Redesdale, father of the 6 Mitford sisters (Nancy, Pamela, Diana, Unity, Jessica and Deborah).
- Mr Bennet, patriarch in *Pride and Prejudice*, father of Jane, Elizabeth (Lizzy), Mary, Kitty and Lydia.
- Tsar Nicholas II, father of Olga, Tatiana, Maria and Anastasia.
- King Lear's daughters were Goneril, Regan and Cordelia.

2 points for the Fire-Eaters against the Clareites, in series 12.

5 points

4: School system

3 points

3: City government

2 points

2: Seaports

?

| 4: School system | 3: City government | 2: Seaports | 1: Drug trade |

Seasons of *The Wire*

Each series of the US drama series *The Wire* was based on a different aspect of life in Baltimore, as listed here

No points for the Technologists or the Analysts here. 'S all in the game …

5 points

Y

3 points

Tb

2 points

Er

?

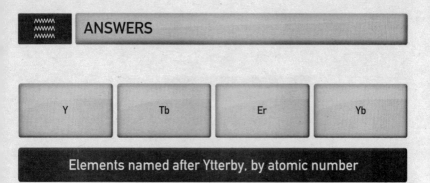

| Y | Tb | Er | Yb |

Elements named after Ytterby, by atomic number

A mine near the village of Ytterby yielded a mineral that eventually revealed four new elements. Ytterby is on the Swedish island Resarö. The tiny quarry in the tiny place is very significant to scientists, as it contained so many rare earth metals (and glaciers had swept away the land above, making it easier to mine them)

- Y: Yttrium (atomic number 39).
- Tb: Terbium (atomic number 65).
- Er: Erbium (atomic number 68).
- Yb: Ytterbium (atomic number 70).

No points for the Korfballers or the Beekeepers here.

Hard to know what to say about this question except, yes, sometimes *Only Connect* is really difficult. Well done if you got it at home.

5 points

China and
Mongolia

3 points

Argentina
and Chile

2 points

Kazakhstan
and Russia

?

| China and Mongolia | Argentina and Chile | Kazakhstan and Russia | USA and Canada |

Longest land borders

- China and Mongolia: 4,677 km.
- Argentina and Chile: 5,308 km.
- Kazakhstan and Russia: 6,846 km.
- USA and Canada: 8,893 km.

The borders don't need to be continuous. The USA/Canada figure includes the Alaska–Canada border.

The Bakers gambled on this in the series 8 final and scored a remarkable 5-pointer. It was still not enough to beat their rivals the Board Gamers though.

Nato	Nerve	Nyssa	Nape
Nipa	Nyet	Nates	Nardo
Nose	Nerine	Ntes	Não
Nej	Nine	Nein	Nettle

CLUE WORDS

In the same group: Ntes and Nine
In the same group: Nein and Não
In the same group: Nates and Nape
In the same group: Nerine and Nettle

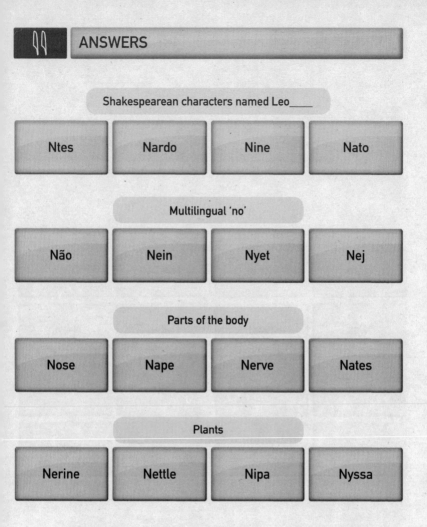

Shakespearean characters named Leo____

| Ntes | Nardo | Nine | Nato |

Multilingual 'no'

| Não | Nein | Nyet | Nej |

Parts of the body

| Nose | Nape | Nerve | Nates |

Plants

| Nerine | Nettle | Nipa | Nyssa |

The *Only Connect* series final often rewards the teams with horrible walls, and this was as nasty as any. The String Section managed 3 points on this, with 1 of those for their last-minute brilliance in spotting the answer to the Shakespeare group.

Māṃsa	Mantis	Matka	Mark
Moeder	Mash	Matsya	Mère
Mink	Madya	Matthew	Martin
Molly	Mudrā	Mutter	Matthias

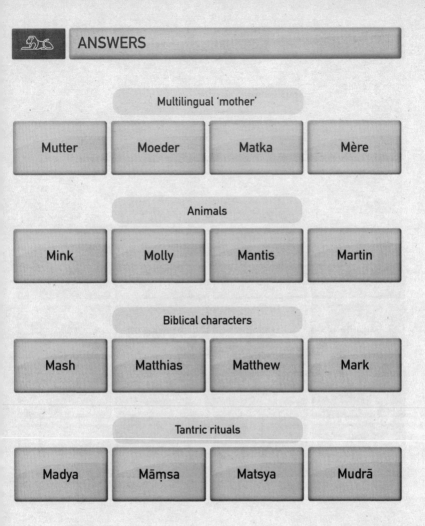

Multilingual 'mother'

| Mutter | Moeder | Matka | Mère |

Animals

| Mink | Molly | Mantis | Martin |

Biblical characters

| Mash | Matthias | Matthew | Mark |

Tantric rituals

| Madya | Māṃsa | Matsya | Mudrā |

This horror was the torture for the other finalists in series 11, the Wayfarers, who eked out a hard-fought 4 points. When the show is recorded, the teams do not see each other's walls. In fact, the first time they see each other's walls is when their show is broadcast. Thus if the walls are paired in some way – like these ones – with similar tricks or types of clues in them, then neither team has an advantage.

Two TV shows concatenated

DC TRWH WN TST BML LNR

THF RSHP RN CFBL RW LF

M GN MPC L DS

MDR NFM LYG Y

Two TV shows concatenated

DC TRWH WN TST BML LNR

DOCTOR WHO WANTS TO BE A MILLIONAIRE?

THF RSHP RN CFBL RW LF

THE FRESH PRINCE OF BEL-AIRWOLF

M GN MPC L DS

MAGNUM PI, CLAUDIUS

MDR NFM LYG Y

MODERN FAMILY GUY

Things a satnav might say

TR NRG HT

TR NR NDW HRPS SBL

NNH ND RDY RDSB RLFT

YHVR CHD YRDS TNTN

Things a satnav might say

TR NRG HT

TURN RIGHT

TR NR NDW HRPS SBL

TURN AROUND WHERE POSSIBLE

NNH ND RDY RDSB RLFT

IN ONE HUNDRED YARDS, BEAR LEFT

YHVR CHD YRDS TNTN

YOU HAVE REACHED YOUR DESTINATION

A social media abbreviation and its meaning

MGN DHM YG D

TMN DTM CHN FRM TN

TL DRN DTLN GDD NTRD

YLN DYN LYL VNC

A social media abbreviation and its meaning

MGN DHM YG D

'OMG' AND OH MY GOD

TMN DTM CHN FRM TN

'TMI' AND TOO MUCH INFORMATION

TL DRN DTLN GDD NTRD

'TL;DR' AND TOO LONG; DIDN'T READ

YLN DYN LYL VNC

'YOLO' AND YOU ONLY LIVE ONCE

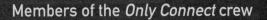

Members of the *Only Connect* crew

DV DTHQ STN DTR

JLT THM KPR TST

HWT HGRP HCSP RTR

HNN HTH SSS TN TPR DCR

Members of the *Only Connect* crew

DV DTHQ STN DTR

DAVID THE QUESTION EDITOR

JLT THM KPR TST

JULIET THE MAKE-UP ARTIST

HWT HGRP HCSP RTR

HUW THE GRAPHICS OPERATOR

HNN HTH SSS TN TPR DCR

HANNAH THE ASSISTANT PRODUCER

This question caused great excitement (and anger!) on Twitter when originally broadcast, though the teams managed just fine. 'How is anybody supposed to know these?', the people shouted? Well, they've been in the credits every week, and in any case, it's just a not-too-difficult word puzzle. Welcome to *Only Connect*.

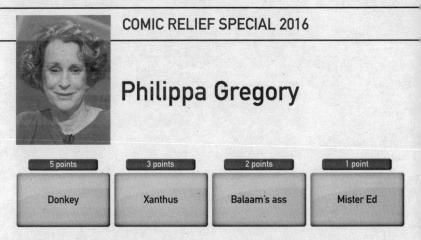

Philippa Gregory

5 points	3 points	2 points	1 point
Donkey	Xanthus	Balaam's ass	Mister Ed

'It was our first question and I had the familiar sense of excitement and dread at doing a TV quiz where if you are an idiot millions of people will know about it (as opposed to usual idiocy which is hopefully private). David Baddiel was team captain, I was on his left, the great Dr John Cooper Clarke on his right. Hang on a minute I said to David Baddiel – these are talking horses. He was as amazed as I was that the answer had fallen into my head. It was so unlikely that the question editor asked me later how I had known that Balaam's Ass had spoken. At last my childhood in the library had paid off. I had read of Balaam in George Eliot, somewhere, God knows why, nor why it stuck in my head. But there it was – the unexpected rewards of scholarship.'

- Mister Ed, in long-running 60s US sitcom the same name
- Balaam's ass, from the Bible, Numbers 22:21-39
- Xanthus, Achilles' wonderful horse, as described in Homer's Iliad
- Donkey, from the Shrek films.

These are all equines from various works who can talk

Meropic equines

BONUS ROUNDS

CONNECTING WALLS

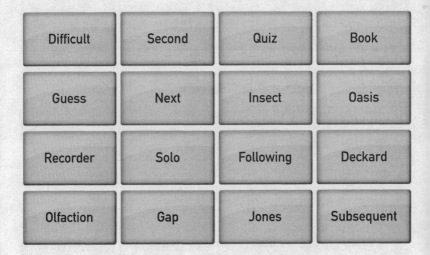

Difficult	Second	Quiz	Book
Guess	Next	Insect	Oasis
Recorder	Solo	Following	Deckard
Olfaction	Gap	Jones	Subsequent

CLUE WORDS

In the same group: Book and Solo

In the same group: Olfaction and Difficult

Not in the same group: Next and Gap

Not in the same group: Following and Insect

End with belief groups

Difficult	Insect	Olfaction	Recorder

Succeeding

Second	Next	Following	Subsequent

Clothing brands

Quiz	Guess	Gap	Oasis

Harrison Ford roles

Book	Solo	Jones	Deckard

Second	Horn	Stocking	Entrance
Tree	Slip	Present	Island
Rib	Carol	Eve	Veil
Nelson	Desert	Card	Noah

CLUE WORDS

In the same group: Rib and Veil

In the same group: Desert and Second

Not in the same group: Eve and Present

Not in the same group: Stocking and Tree

Trevors

| Eve | Horn | Noah | Nelson |

Christmas ____

| Tree | Carol | Card | Island |

Knitting stitches

| Rib | Slip | Veil | Stocking |

Different stress gives different meanings

| Entrance | Desert | Second | Present |

Anagram	Morse	Wright	Green Cross
Post	Acrostic	Highway	Montalbano
Rebus	Dress	Luther	Cryptogram
Earhart	Gently	Jumble	Lindbergh

CLUE WORDS

In the same group: Post and Lindbergh
In the same group: Dress and Green Cross
Not in the same group: Morse and Montalbano
Not in the same group: Rebus and Acrostic

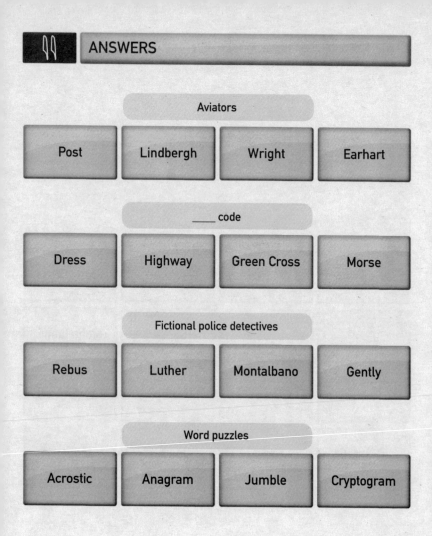

Aviators

| Post | Lindbergh | Wright | Earhart |

_____ code

| Dress | Highway | Green Cross | Morse |

Fictional police detectives

| Rebus | Luther | Montalbano | Gently |

Word puzzles

| Acrostic | Anagram | Jumble | Cryptogram |

Brass	Schirra	Wedding	Bacon
Carpenter	Dough	Grissom	Gastric
Lolly	Stokes	Wonga	Shepard
Rubber	Glenn	Alice	Willows

CLUE WORDS

In the same group: Schirra and Glenn

In the same group: Willows and Stokes

Not in the same group: Grissom and Glenn

Not in the same group: Brass and Wonga

Characters from *CSI*

Stokes | Brass | Grissom | Willows

Mercury project astronauts

Glenn | Shepard | Carpenter | Schirra

Slang for money

Lolly | Bacon | Dough | Wonga

_____ band

Wedding | Alice | Rubber | Gastric

Toffee	Moth	Rainbow	Tablet
Darn	Ranger	Freaking	Curve
Brownie	Shoot	Fudge	Basket
Meat	Bonbon	Senior	Screw

CLUE WORDS
In the same group: Senior and Ranger
In the same group: Screw and Curve
Not in the same group: Basket and Moth
Not in the same group: Brownie and Toffee

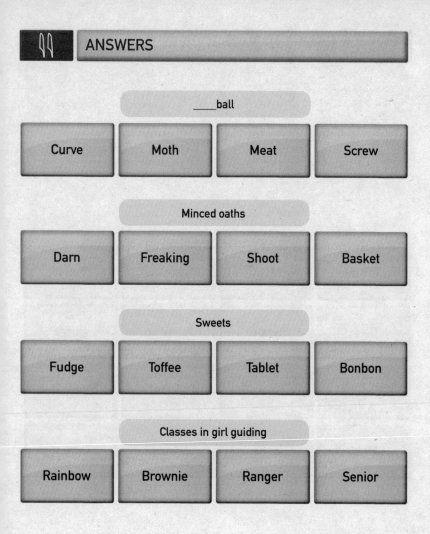

_____ball

| Curve | Moth | Meat | Screw |

Minced oaths

| Darn | Freaking | Shoot | Basket |

Sweets

| Fudge | Toffee | Tablet | Bonbon |

Classes in girl guiding

| Rainbow | Brownie | Ranger | Senior |

Perfect	Boxer	Don't	Sing
Bermuda	Zucchini	Fever	Sidewalk
Shape of You	Board	Drugstore	The A Team
Rugby	Cotton candy	Elevator	Cargo

CLUE WORDS

In the same group: Fever and Rugby

In the same group: Bermuda and Boxer

Not in the same group: Perfect and Sing

Not in the same group: Sidewalk and Elevator

ANSWERS

Ed Sheeran songs

| Don't | The A Team | Shape of You | Sing |

_____ pitch

| Perfect | Fever | Rugby | Elevator |

Different in American English

| Sidewalk | Cotton candy | Drugstore | Zucchini |

Types of shorts

| Bermuda | Cargo | Boxer | Board |

Keith Richards	Rolling Stone	Q	Pingu
Tux	Way	Clash	Wheezy
Paddington	Mojo	Nerve	Mumble
Marbles	Peso	Uncut	Perspective

CLUE WORDS

In the same group: Peso and Wheezy

In the same group: Keith Richards and Paddington

Not in the same group: Rolling Stone and Clash

Not in the same group: Q and Mojo

Fictional penguins

Mumble	Peso	Tux	Wheezy

Ben Whishaw roles

Q	Paddington	Pingu	Keith Richards

Music magazines

Rolling Stone	Clash	Uncut	Mojo

Lose your _____

Way	Marbles	Nerve	Perspective

Mason	Gap	Dean	Beer
Nice	English	Sweat	Nancy
Carpenter	Coburn	Dijon	Caan
Tours	Honey	Cagney	Wholegrain

CLUE WORDS

In the same group: Gap and Nice

In the same group: Carpenter and Honey

Not in the same group: Mason and Cagney

Not in the same group: Dijon and Nancy

ANSWERS

Mustards

Dijon | English | Beer | Wholegrain

Types of bee

Carpenter | Sweat | Mason | Honey

Actors named James

Coburn | Caan | Cagney | Dean

Capitals of French departments

Nice | Gap | Tours | Nancy

Welsh	Angels	Angles	Grahame
Rankin	Liver	Ballantyne	Freedom
Strong	University graduates	Supreme	Ponty
Burns	Black	Stevenson	Feel

CLUE WORDS

In the same group: Liver and Ponty
In the same group: Angles and University graduates
Not in the same group: Welsh and Rankin
Not in the same group: Freedom and Angels

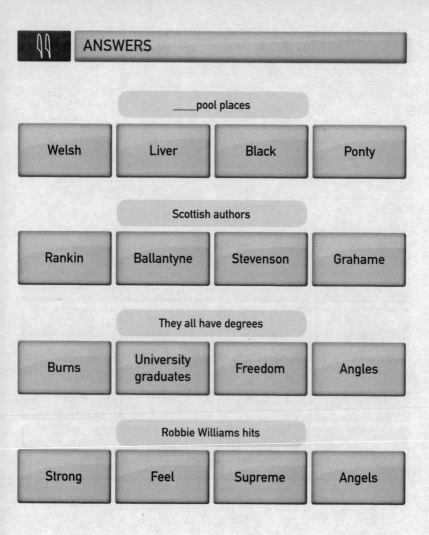

_____pool places

| Welsh | Liver | Black | Ponty |

Scottish authors

| Rankin | Ballantyne | Stevenson | Grahame |

They all have degrees

| Burns | University graduates | Freedom | Angles |

Robbie Williams hits

| Strong | Feel | Supreme | Angels |

Mouse	Combination	Place	Caterpillar
Chubb	Beer	Pat	Welcome
Hatter	Cylinder	Tuner	Dead bolt
Soul	Gym	Mortice	Mock Turtle

CLUE WORDS

In the same group: Pat and Mock Turtle

In the same group: Tuner and Soul

Not in the same group: Chubb and Dead bolt

Not in the same group: Place and Welcome

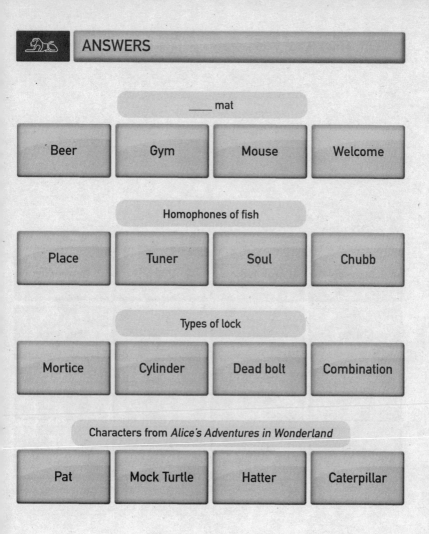

_____ mat

| Beer | Gym | Mouse | Welcome |

Homophones of fish

| Place | Tuner | Soul | Chubb |

Types of lock

| Mortice | Cylinder | Dead bolt | Combination |

Characters from *Alice's Adventures in Wonderland*

| Pat | Mock Turtle | Hatter | Caterpillar |

The Kiss	Hex	Best Mate	Shogi
Long Run	Eternal Springtime	Abalone	The Gates of Hell
Go	Norton's Coin	Man with the Broken Nose	Orac
The Thinker	Othello	Holly	The Fellow

CLUE WORDS

In the same group: Long Run and Norton's Coin

In the same group: Holly and Orac

Not in the same group: The Kiss and The Thinker

Not in the same group: Hex and Go

Strategy board games

| Go | Othello | Abalone | Shogi |

Works by Rodin

| The Kiss | Eternal Springtime | The Gates of Hell | Man with the Broken Nose |

Fictional computers

| Hex | The Thinker | Holly | Orac |

Cheltenham Gold Cup winners

| Long Run | Norton's Coin | The Fellow | Best Mate |

Flange	Belly	Coogan	Ballcock
Beam	Spigot	Truss	Schneider
Front	Suspension	Tank	Morris
Swing	Marber	Tap	Cantilever

CLUE WORDS

In the same group: Tank and Spigot

In the same group: Front and Coogan

Not in the same group: Tap and Ballcock

Not in the same group: Swing and Cantilever

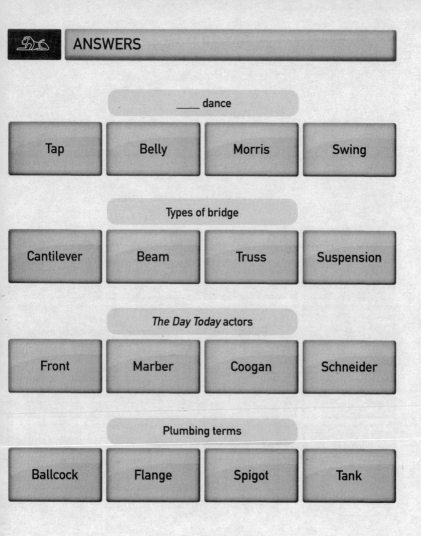

_____ dance

| Tap | Belly | Morris | Swing |

Types of bridge

| Cantilever | Beam | Truss | Suspension |

The Day Today actors

| Front | Marber | Coogan | Schneider |

Plumbing terms

| Ballcock | Flange | Spigot | Tank |

Pizza	Bugs	Damp squib	Baby Face
Let Down	Fan	Flukey	Creep
Dutch	Dud	Reckoner	Convection
Lucky	Bummer	Beehive	Bathos

CLUE WORDS

In the same group: Beehive and Fan
In the same group: Baby Face and Dutch
Not in the same group: Let Down and Damp squib
Not in the same group: Flukey and Lucky

Anticlimax

Bathos	Bummer	Damp squib	Dud

Radiohead songs

Let Down	Lucky	Creep	Reckoner

US gangster nicknames

Baby Face	Dutch	Bugs	Flukey

_____ oven

Fan	Convection	Pizza	Beehive

Dial	Basildon	Baby	Stripe
Pocket	PayPal	Chakra	Tilbury
Sage	Miniature	Chigwell	Sister
Dwarf	Grays	Braintree	Toy

CLUE WORDS

In the same group: Chakra and Dial

In the same group: PayPal and Stripe

Not in the same group: Dwarf and Miniature

Not in the same group: Braintree and Basildon

Online payment providers

| Braintree | PayPal | Sage | Stripe |

Places in Essex

| Basildon | Chigwell | Grays | Tilbury |

Things that come in sevens

| Chakra | Dial | Dwarf | Sister |

Synonyms for small

| Baby | Miniature | Pocket | Toy |

John	Bog	Town	Lindsey
Mick	Head	Stevie	Style
Privy	Christine	Vatican	Kent
Wessex	Security	Mercia	Jacks

CLUE WORDS
In the same group: Lindsey and Kent
In the same group: Mick and Christine
Not in the same group: John and Bog
Not in the same group: Privy and Style

Anglo-Saxon kingdoms

| Kent | Mercia | Wessex | Lindsey |

Fleetwood Mac members

| Mick | Christine | John | Stevie |

Words for toilet

| Jacks | Bog | Head | Privy |

_____ Council

| Town | Security | Vatican | Style |

Electric	Crud	Cromarty	Cerulean
Solway	Sand	Sky	Conger
Baby	Pentland	Firn	Cornflower
Dornoch	Powder	Moray	Slush

CLUE WORDS

In the same group: Conger and Sand

In the same group: Crud and Powder

Not in the same group: Moray and Solway

Not in the same group: Electric and Sky

_____ eel

| Conger | Electric | Moray | Sand |

Firths

| Dornoch | Solway | Cromarty | Pentland |

Shades of blue

| Baby | Cerulean | Sky | Cornflower |

Types of snow

| Powder | Slush | Crud | Firn |

Tonight	Sheep	Korea	Maria
Living	Dakota	Somewhere	Sports
America	Cinema	Shields	I Feel Pretty
Magic	A Boy Like That	Market	Atlantic

CLUE WORDS

- In the same group: Magic and Sheep
- In the same group: Sports and Living
- Not in the same group: America and Tonight
- Not in the same group: Atlantic and Dakota

Songs from *West Side Story*

| A Boy Like That | Tonight | I Feel Pretty | Somewhere |

North and South places

| America | Dakota | Korea | Shields |

Black _____

| Maria | Market | Magic | Sheep |

Sky TV channels

| Atlantic | Sports | Cinema | Living |

Pleasant	Mary	Fantastic	Fate
Rushmore	Bottle	Moira	Carmel
Doom	Sinai	Gilbert	Moonrise
Isle	Gloria	Kismet	Gisela

First word of Wes Anderson film titles

Bottle	Isle	Fantastic	Moonrise

Mount _____

Rushmore	Pleasant	Sinai	Carmel

Destiny

Doom	Moira	Kismet	Fate

Stuarts

Mary	Gloria	Gilbert	Gisela

Clog	Galosh	Mandrake	Pendennis
Dempster	Windsor	Chopine	Choke
Moccasin	Snag	Sandal	Hickey
Corfe	Pandora	Bar	Espadrille

CLUE WORDS

In the same group: Chopine and Galosh

In the same group: Sandal and Corfe

Not in the same group: Clog and Moccasin

Not in the same group: Pendennis and Dempster

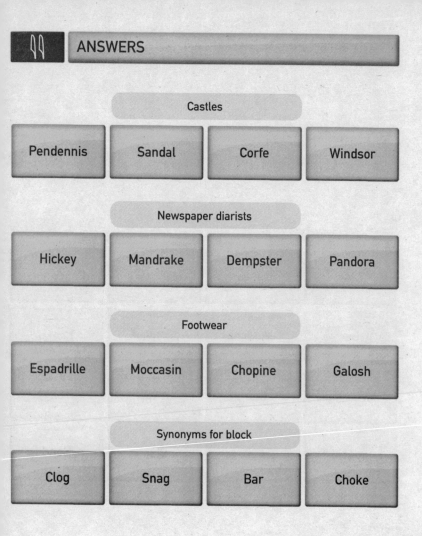

Castles

| Pendennis | Sandal | Corfe | Windsor |

Newspaper diarists

| Hickey | Mandrake | Dempster | Pandora |

Footwear

| Espadrille | Moccasin | Chopine | Galosh |

Synonyms for block

| Clog | Snag | Bar | Choke |

Hand	Break	Iso	Craft
Foot	Hand	Fright	Tor
Abut	Leg up	Hand	League
Coach	Rod	Clue	Hand

CLUE WORDS

In the same group: Clue and Break

In the same group: Craft and Coach

In the same group: Iso and Abut

Not in the same group: Hand and Hand and Hand and Hand and Hand and Hand

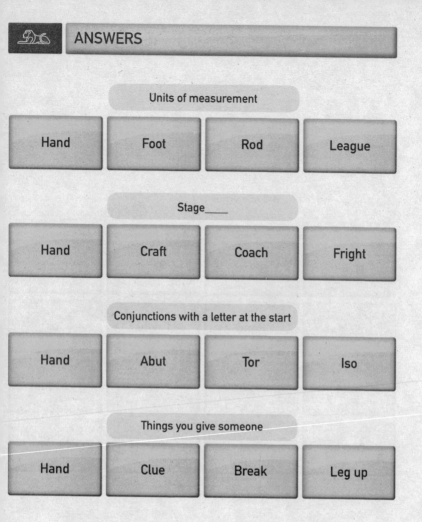

Units of measurement

| Hand | Foot | Rod | League |

Stage____

| Hand | Craft | Coach | Fright |

Conjunctions with a letter at the start

| Hand | Abut | Tor | Iso |

Things you give someone

| Hand | Clue | Break | Leg up |

A gimmick wall, which could be a bit unfair on the contestants if used on the show. Hopefully you worked out easily enough (or used the clue to work out) that the 'Hands' all had to be in different groups.

BONUS ROUNDS

MISSING VOWELS

Eighties rock bands with one letter changed

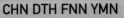

CHN DTH FNN YMN

T HCR D

THS TKR SS

TRSF RBRS

Eighties rock bands with one letter changed

CHN DTH FNN YMN

ECHO AND THE FUNNYMEN

T HCR D

THE CURD

THS TKR SS

THE STOKE ROSES

TRSF RBRS

TEARS FOR BEARS

- Echo and the Bunnymen.
- The Cure.
- The Stone Roses.
- Tears for Fears.

Things that there are Royal Societies for

THP RVN TN FCR LTYTN MLS

PB LCH LTH

T HPR VNT NFCC DNTS

B LN DCH LD RN

Things that there are Royal Societies for

THP RVN TN FCR LTYTN MLS

THE PREVENTION OF CRUELTY TO ANIMALS

PB LCH LTH

PUBLIC HEALTH

T HPR VNT NFCC DNTS

THE PREVENTION OF ACCIDENTS

B LN DCH LD RN

BLIND CHILDREN

Soap matriarchs and their soaps

HL NDN LSN DNG HBRS

NNS G DNN DMM RDL

PP PF LTC HRN DH MN DWY

NS HR PLSN DCRN TNST RT

Soap matriarchs and their soaps

HL NDN LSN DNG HBRS

HELEN DANIELS AND NEIGHBOURS

NNS G DNN DMM RDL

ANNIE SUGDEN AND EMMERDALE

PP PF LTC HRN DH MN DWY

PIPPA FLETCHER AND HOME AND AWAY

NS HR PLSN DCRN TNST RT

ENA SHARPLES AND CORONATION STREET

Jobs George Osborne has had

DT RFTH VN NGST NDRD

M PF RTTT N

SH DWC HNCL LRF THXC HQR

CH RFT HN RTHR NPW RHSP RTN RSHP

ANSWERS

Jobs George Osborne has had

DT RFTH VN NGST NDRD

EDITOR OF THE EVENING STANDARD

M PF RTTT N

MP FOR TATTON

SH DWC HNCL LRF THXC HQR

SHADOW CHANCELLOR OF THE EXCHEQUER

CH RFT HN RTHR NPW RHSP RTN RSHP

CHAIR OF THE NORTHERN POWERHOUSE PARTNERSHIP

Symbols and what they mean

H RTN DLV

DT TNDR PT

GR NC RSS NDP HR MCY

MP RS NDNDND

Symbols and what they mean

H RTN DLV

HEART AND LOVE

DT TNDR PT

DITTO AND REPEAT

GR NC RSS NDP HR MCY

GREEN CROSS AND PHARMACY

MP RS NDNDND

AMPERSAND AND AND

Authors merged with comedy characters

RY MN DCHN DLRB NG

M NC LG

LZ BTHD VDB RNT

VR GNW LFS MTH

Authors merged with comedy characters

RY MN DCHN DLRB NG

RAYMOND CHANDLER BING

M NC LG

MONICA ALI G

LZ BTHD VDB RNT

ELIZABETH DAVID BRENT

VR GNW LFS MTH

VIRGINIA WOOLFIE SMITH

Countries and the first lines of their national anthems

NT DSTT SFM RCN DSY CN YS BYT HDWN SRLYL GHT

F RNC NDL LNSN FNTS DLP TR

S PNN D

C NDN DCN D

Countries and the first lines of their national anthems

NT DSTT SFM RCN DSY CN YS BYT HDWN SRLYL GHT

UNITED STATES OF AMERICA AND
O SAY CAN YOU SEE BY THE DAWN'S EARLY LIGHT

F RNC NDL LNSN FNTS DLP TR

FRANCE AND ALLONS ENFANTS DE LA PATRIE

S PNN D

SPAIN AND

C NDN DCN D

CANADA AND O CANADA

- Spain's national anthem, 'Marcha Real', currently does not have any official lyrics.
- Both English and French versions start with 'O Canada'.

Quotations from the works of Edward Bulwer-Lytton

TH PNS MGHT RTH NTHS WRD

T HG RTNW SHD

TW SDR KNDS TRM YNG HT

RVL TN SRN TMD WTHR SWTR

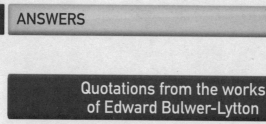

Quotations from the works of Edward Bulwer-Lytton

TH PNS MGHT RTH NTHS WRD

THE PEN IS MIGHTIER THAN THE SWORD

T HG RTNW SHD

THE GREAT UNWASHED

TW SDR KNDS TRM YNG HT

IT WAS A DARK AND STORMY NIGHT (or 'TWAS A ...)

RVL TN SRN TMD WTHR SWTR

REVOLUTIONS ARE NOT MADE WITH ROSEWATER

- Edward Bulwer-Lytton is a classic case where the quotations are more famous than the person who came up with them.

Phrases in clickbait titles

YW NTB LV

WL LCH NGY RLF

SGNSYRCTLLY

W THTH SN WR DTR CK

Phrases in clickbait titles

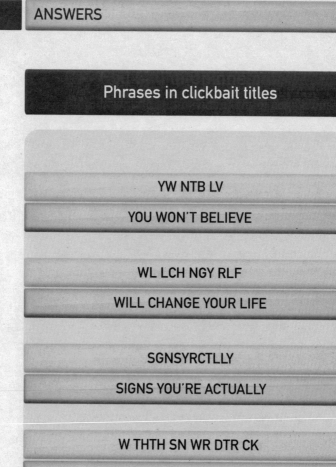

YW NTB LV

YOU WON'T BELIEVE

WL LCH NGY RLF

WILL CHANGE YOUR LIFE

SGNSYRCTLLY

SIGNS YOU'RE ACTUALLY

W THTH SN WR DTR CK

WITH THIS ONE WEIRD TRICK

Shakespeare characters and their killers

HM LTN DLR TS

DN CNN DMC BTH

DS DMN NDT HLL

MR CTN DTY BLT

Shakespeare characters and their killers

HM LTN DLR TS

HAMLET AND LAERTES

DN CNN DMC BTH

DUNCAN AND MACBETH

DS DMN NDT HLL

DESDEMONA AND OTHELLO

MR CTN DTY BLT

MERCUTIO AND TYBALT

Seventh films in franchises

S TRW RST HFR CWK NS

NH RMJ ST YSSC RTS RVC

CR RYNC BBY

PL CCD MY MSS NTMS CW

Seventh films in franchises

S TRW RST HFR CWK NS

STAR WARS: THE FORCE AWAKENS

NH RMJ ST YSSC RTS RVC

ON HER MAJESTY'S SECRET SERVICE

CR RYNC BBY

CARRY ON CABBY

PL CCD MY MSS NTMS CW

POLICE ACADEMY: MISSION TO MOSCOW

Football managers and their coinages

JSM RN HNDP RKTH BS

GR MTY LRN DDN TLK THT

ND WNDB NCB CKB LTY

LXF R GS NNDS QK YBM TM

Football managers and their coinages

JSM RN HNDP RKTH BS

JOSE MOURINHO AND PARK THE BUS

GR MTY LRN DDN TLK THT

GRAHAM TAYLOR AND DO I NOT LIKE THAT

ND WNDB NCB CKB LTY

IAIN DOWIE AND BOUNCEBACKABILITY

LXF R GS NNDS QK YBM TM

ALEX FERGUSON AND SQUEAKY BUM TIME

TV shows merged with computer games

CRNT NSTR TFG HTR

DR PTH DDD NKY KNG

WS TWR LDFW RC RFT

S PT TNGM GFM PRS

TV shows merged with computer games

CRNT NSTR TFG HTR

CORONATION STREETFIGHTER

DR PTH DDD NKY KNG

DROP THE DEAD DONKEY KONG

WS TWR LDFW RC RFT

WESTWORLD OF WARCRAFT

S PT TNGM GFM PRS

SPITTING IMAGE OF EMPIRES

Commonly paired words replaced by homophones

LC HN DQ Y

WNDY

NNN DW T

B RDN DJ MB

Commonly paired words replaced by homophones

LC HN DQ Y

LOCH AND QUAY

WNDY

EWE AND EYE

NNN DW T

INN AND OWT

B RDN DJ MB

BRED AND JAMB

Similes in songs

YLV DYR LFL KCN DL NTHW ND

MLK B RD

LKB RD GVRT RBL DWT R WLLLY MDW N

KL MN JRR SSLK LYM PSB VT HSR NGT

Similes in songs

YLV DYR LFL KCN DL NTHW ND

YOU LIVED YOUR LIFE LIKE A CANDLE IN THE WIND

MLK B RD

I'M LIKE A BIRD

LKB RD GVRT RBL DWT R WLLLY MDW N

LIKE A BRIDGE OVER TROUBLED WATER
I WILL LAY ME DOWN

KL MN JRR SSLK LYM PSB VT HSR NGT

KILIMANJARO RISES LIKE OLYMPUS
ABOVE THE SERENGETI

- Elton John.
- Nelly Furtado.
- Simon & Garfunkel.
- Toto.

Cops and robbers

LTN SSN DLC PN

JH NMC CLNN DH NSGR BR

NS PC TRJ VRTN DJN VL JN

JC KSL PPRN DRN NBG GS

Cops and robbers

LTN SSN DLC PN

ELIOT NESS AND AL CAPONE

JH NMC CLNN DH NSGR BR

JOHN MCCLANE AND HANS GRUBER

NS PC TRJ VRTN DJN VL JN

INSPECTOR JAVERT AND JEAN VALJEAN

JC KSL PPRN DRN NBG GS

JACK SLIPPER AND RONNIE BIGGS

Replacement for swearwords in films

ML NFR MR

FRG TY

YFR YGDM THR

SNF SQD

Replacement for swearwords in films

ML NFR MR

MELON FARMER

FRG TY

FORGET YOU

YFR YGDM THR

YOU FAIRY GODMOTHER

SNF SQD

SON OF A SQUID

A character and what they metamorphose
into in Ovid's *Metamorphoses*

DNSN DFL WR

RCH NND SP DR

CTN NDS TG

NRC SSS NDN RC SSS

A character and what they metamorphose into in Ovid's *Metamorphoses*

DNSN DFL WR

ADONIS AND A FLOWER

RCH NND SP DR

ARACHNE AND A SPIDER

CTN NDS TG

ACTAEON AND A STAG

NRC SSS NDN RC SSS

NARCISSUS AND A NARCISSUS

Shops merged with countries

TS CTL ND

BN TTN G

J JMM NBB LGM

LK LND RR

Shops merged with countries

TS CTL ND

TESCOTLAND

BN TTN G

BENETTONGA

J JMM NBB LGM

JOJO MAMAN BEBELGIUM

LK LND RR

LAKELANDORRA

Pairs of expressions that could almost mean the same thing

TMMC HNN DLR MCL CK

PH RMCS TND RG DLR

PR TYR NGN DSC LCR CL

BKF RND RDN GFS TVL

Pairs of expressions that could almost mean the same thing

TMMC HNN DLR MCL CK

TIME MACHINE AND ALARM CLOCK

PH RMCS TND DRG DLR

PHARMACIST AND DRUG DEALER

PR TYR NGN DSC LCR CL

PARTY RING AND SOCIAL CIRCLE

BKF RND RDN GFS TVL

BOOK FAIR AND READING FESTIVAL

Facts and Figures

All stats relate to series 1–14 of *Only Connect*.

Contestants and Teams

Number of shows: **308**
including all specials and 4 Wall Night Specials

232 Number of teams

Number of different individuals appearing on the show: **677**

19 contestants (mainly special guest quizzers) have played for two different teams

Roll Call of Champions

Bold indicates a champions of champions winner.

Team	Series	Played	Won	Points per game	Points per R1	Points per R2	Points per R3	Points per R4
Crossworders[1]	1	8	8	25.4	4.3	7.3	8.5	5.4
Rugby Boys	2	4	3	20.8	4.3	4.3	7.8	4.5
Gamblers	3	5	4	25.6	5.4	5.6	8.2	6.4
Epicureans[2]	4	6	5	26.7	3.5	4.2	6.8	12.2
Analysts	5	5	4	22.2	4.2	4.2	8.0	5.8
Scribes[3]	6	5	5	24.8	5.6	3.6	8.2	7.4
Francophiles	7	4	4	25.0	3.5	6.3	8.3	7.0
Board Gamers[4]	8	5	4	23.4	3.6	6.2	5.8	7.8
Europhiles	9	5	4	15.0	2.0	3.0	4.2	5.8
Orienteers	10	5	5	24.4	3.8	5.8	8.2	6.6
String Section[5]	11	6	6	20.2	3.0	4.5	7.0	5.7
Verbivores[6]	12	8	6	21.8	3.9	5.8	5.8	6.4
Escapologists[7]	13	8	6	21.8	3.5	5.5	5.9	6.9
Dicers	14	5	5	23.8	3.0	6.6	9.4	4.8

Note 1: The Crossworders played and won 4 games to win series 1. They have additionally beaten the Rugby Boys in a Champions of Champions match, the Epicureans in a Champions of Champions of Champions match, a team of *University Challenge* champions from Emmanuel College, Cambridge, and a team of *Mastermind* champions.

Note 2: The Epicureans played 4 games to win series 4, and additionally beat the Gamblers in a Champions of Champions match before losing to the Crossworders in a Champions of Champions of Champions match.

Note 3: The Scribes played and won 4 games to win series 6, and additionally beat the Analysts in a Champions of Champions match.

Note 4: The Board Gamers were the first team to win a series having lost a match, to the Lasletts.

Note 5: The String Section played and won 5 games to win series 11, and additionally beat the Europhiles in a Champions of Champions match.

Note 6: In the first 37 show series, the Verbivores became champions despite losing two matches, but they avenged both defeats later in the tournament.

Note 7: The Escapologists became champions despite two narrow defeats, both of which they avenged later in the tournament including vs the Belgophiles in the final.

Scores

Average score for each team in one game:

19.98

Average for R1: **3.7**

Average for R2: **4.1**

Average for R3: **7.1**

Average for R4: **5.1**

41 Highest ever score by a team:
by the Epicureans in series 4

Highest aggregate score: **63** in Epicureans (41)
vs Courtiers (22) in series 4

Round 1: Connections

12

Highest individual team score on R1: points by the Alesmen in series 4 when it was 12–0 after R1 in their match against the Pool Sharks. The Alesmen won 33–28.

Highest aggregate score on R1: **16** points in a Comic Relief special when it was 8–8 after R1 between Treesome (Brian Sewell, Adam Hart-Davis, Grub Smith) and Larks (Michael Bywater, Andrew Motion, Stuart Maconie)

14 5-pointers scored on R1

Average score on a R1 question: **1.24**

1.11 points

Average score on R1 music questions

R1 music questions that go unanswered by either team: **23%**

1.14

Average score on R1 picture questions

R1 picture questions that go unanswered by either team: **28%**

455

Round 2: Sequences

Highest individual team score on R2: **11** points by the Board Gamers vs the Globetrotters in series 8.

Highest aggregate score on R2: **16** points between the Globetrotters (5) and the Board Gamers (11)

5-pointers scored on R2: **20**

1.35 Average score on a R2 question

Average score on R2 music questions: **1.46**

R2 music questions that go unanswered by either team: **20%**

Average score on R2 picture questions: **1.3**

32% R2 picture questions that go unanswered by either team

Round 3: Connecting Walls

2.3 Average difference in Wall scores

Shows in which there is no difference in Wall scores:
28.7%

Biggest ever difference in Wall scores:
(when the Verbivores got 1 and the
Taverners got 10. The Verbivores still
won by overturning a 6-point deficit
going into Vowels)

9

1

Lowest ever Wall score
– achieved twice, once
by the Verbivores and
once by the Second Violinists

Round 4: Missing Vowels

10.4 Average number of points added on Vowels

Number of 'come from behind' victories on Vowels: **47**

How often teams 'come from behind' to win on Vowels: **15.5%** , i.e. once every 6 to 7 games

Largest ever Vowels turnaround: **7** points by the Verbivores in series 12. They also have the second highest turnaround of 6 points

7-point turnaround: **1**

6-point turnaround: **1**

5-point turnaround: **2**

4-point turnaround: **9**

3-point turnaround: **7**

2-point turnaround: **13**

1-point turnaround: **14**

Number of games resolved by a tie-break: **17**

Acknowledgements

Jack, David and Victoria would like to thank:
The BBC, Ben Beech, David J. Bodycombe, Adam Bostock-Smith, Jeff Bowman, Chris Cadenne, Steve Castle, Rob Cawdery, Sarah Clay, Alan Connor, Gethin Davies, Hannah-Jane Davies, Janice Hadlow, Gilly Hall, Jon Harvey, Jenny Heap, Llŷr Hughes, Rachel Hunter Hamilton, Peter Jamieson, Ben Jones, Siân G. Lloyd, Sara Low, Charlotte Macdonald, Rhiannon Murphy, Daniel Peake, Shaun Pye, RDF, Huw Rhys, Chris and Megan Stuart, Claire Tatham, Rob Thomas, Mike Turner, Alan Tyler, Howard Watson, Hywel Williams and all the crew in Cardiff, all the contestants who have ever come along to play, and all our wonderful question writers, in particular those not mentioned above whose questions appear in the book:

Jonathan Broad, Mark Burgin, Guy Campbell, Elise Czajkowski, Jim Fishwick, Jonathan and Rozann Gilbert, Tony Gold, Jamie Hall, Jonathan Henderson, Wei-Hwa Huang, Philip Marlow, Dave Mattingly, Alex McMillan, Chris Miller (KM), Richard Osman, Tony Rubin, Hugh Rycroft, Smylers, Laura Watson, Geraldine Wiley, Teri Wilson